The Art of *Letting Go* To *Glow*

An Artistic Guide to
Emotional Creativity
-Born in The Wilderness

Jeffrey Bryan Grubert

The Art of Letting Go To Glow © Copyright 2025 Jeffrey Bryan Grubert

All rights reserved. No part of this publication may be reproduced, distributed or transmitted in any form or by any means, including photocopying, recording, or other electronic or mechanical methods, without the prior written permission of the publisher, except in the case of brief quotations embodied in critical reviews and certain other noncommercial uses permitted by copyright law.

Although the author and publisher have made every effort to ensure that the information in this book was correct at press time, the author and publisher do not assume and hereby disclaim any liability to any party for any loss, damage, or disruption caused by errors or omissions, whether such errors or omissions result from negligence, accident, or any other cause.

Adherence to all applicable laws and regulations, including international, federal, state and local governing professional licensing, business practices, advertising, and all other aspects of doing business in the US, Canada or any other jurisdiction is the sole responsibility of the reader and consumer.

Neither the author nor the publisher assumes any responsibility or liability whatsoever on behalf of the consumer or reader of this material. Any perceived slight of any individual or organization is purely unintentional.

The resources in this book are provided for informational purposes only and should not be used to replace the specialized training and professional judgment of a health care or mental health care professional.

Neither the author nor the publisher can be held responsible for the use of the information provided within this book. Please always consult a trained professional before making any decision regarding treatment of yourself or others.

ISBN: 979-8-89694-408-9 - eBook
ISBN: 979-8-89694-409-6 - Paperback
ISBN: 979-8-89694-410-2 - Hardcover

CONTENTS

Part One: You Are an Artist: A Human Fact 13
First Steps Into Aquarius 19
    Brushstroke Stars   https://www.youtube.com/shorts/ovKf5Whuf9A
    Glow West 21
    Animate Riddles   https://youtube.com/shorts/meOWd9LEwdU
    River Tree 23
    Grief River   https://youtube.com/shorts/Q076Mi3EUQc
    Glow Turtles 25
    Breath Rhythm   https://youtube.com/shorts/RXDNTig_lV8
    Have Fun 27
    Color Psalm   https://youtube.com/shorts/9-w_p6H7WMo
    The Solar Life 29
    Filtering Light   https://www.youtube.com/shorts/m_MjI250Enw
    Emergence 31
    Threshold Canvas   https://youtube.com/shorts/UdixT7EyveY

Part Two: The Wanderer or Escapist - Unearthing the Gifts of Emotion 33
    The Cosmic Christ 37
    Death's New Face   https://youtube.com/shorts/XQiAK5PsC2A
    Peace & Love in the Bedroom 39
    Canvas Mirror   https://youtube.com/shorts/bZ7xyr1TfmQ
    Free Yourself 41
    Earth Courage   https://youtube.com/shorts/DGSVv5mFN4Q
    Visualize Your Dreams 43
    Descent Ascension   https://youtube.com/shorts/20HOCozf5EE
    Surrender To Win 45
    Pulse Connection   https://www.youtube.com/shorts/W7T8rObBn1M
    Simply Complicated 47
    Holy Ground   https://youtube.com/shorts/AjFxzNJXGLg
    Fly Grounded 49
    Bare Wild   https://youtube.com/shorts/xKkNgoE7Kog

Part Three: Waking up in the Prison of Your Mind 51
Glow Butte Bird 57
Soul Soil   https://youtube.com/shorts/NXf07H6Bomc
Whirlwind 59
Breathing Art

Silly Putty Glow Dog		61
Compost Creation	https://youtube.com/shorts/CpXB6a7ibks	
Glow Jo		63
Light Alchemy	https://www.youtube.com/shorts/VjSTbrfF0Kw	
Flower Bliss		65
Earth's Secrets	https://www.youtube.com/shorts/U4mP_zjyYr0	
Goddess of Light & Dark		67
Sky Lesson	https://youtube.com/shorts/QcwAUXJZEe0	
West		69
Ash Ember	https://youtube.com/shorts/VKQHqATLL4s	
Mighty Glow Bird		71
Absence Cradle	https://youtube.com/shorts/Irt9oSGWfaI	

Part Four: Breathing Through the Storm 73

Haunted Forest		79
Wilderness Studio	https://youtube.com/shorts/ZI2 feu 04MY	
Strawberry Moon		81
Glowing Edges	https://www.youtube.com/shorts/ovKf5Whuf9A	
Glow Stone Lake		83
Sacred Ground	https://www.youtube.com/shorts/LQVaCskVBaw	
Beauty of Chaos		85
Lost Sacred	https://www.youtube.com/shorts/7PuH119mP5A	
SWOOSH!		87
Hollow Reed	https://youtube.com/shorts/__J3PHDa1ug	
From Me to You		89
Ancient Gestures	https://www.youtube.com/shorts/oiOTVcI1xtM	
Peace Now		91
Echo Canyon	https://youtube.com/shorts/JnFC050C5Us	

Part Five: The Dance of Emotions: Understanding the Essential Role of Both Positive and Negative Feelings 93

Sassy Nest		101
Spiral Trust	https://youtube.com/shorts/fub69ndiyG0	
Grow To Glow		103
Loss Geometry	https://youtube.com/shorts/zzzJnT9SUEA	
Birds of Paradise		105
Vessel Pouring	https://youtube.com/shorts/ha4IZFc7ieQ	
Glow Guardian		107
Trembling Trust	https://youtube.com/shorts/_8KIEf-iHH4	
Rio (1 of 3)		109
Of Stones and Storms	https://youtube.com/shorts/aCqMiycCiy0	

De (2 of 3 Rio Series)		111
Earth Holding	https://youtube.com/shorts/lajwIUkAd0o	
Janeiro (3 of 3 Rio Series)		113
Open Hands	https://youtube.com/shorts/0S-cKidQmXU	
Kauai Night Flight		115
Uprooted and Reconnected	https://youtube.com/shorts/LrSTHhTlaMI	

Part Six: The Art of Emotion: How Embracing Feelings Fuels Creativity and an Extraordinary Life 117

Folly of War		123
Sacral Response	https://youtube.com/shorts/QVB3NB2eX84	
Fortune Fish		125
Breath Connection	https://youtube.com/shorts/CVRDAxEi8Bk	
Sedona Glow Bird		127
Heartbeat Silence in Flight	https://youtube.com/shorts/BfkIm8EH7N4	
The Web of Life		129
Spiral Dance	https://youtube.com/shorts/bf01VpYvn60	
Gratitude Glow Garden		131
Broken Branch Homes	https://www.youtube.com/shorts/utt1HQprLuw	
Sweet Darkness		133
Darkness: A Training Ground	https://www.youtube.com/shorts/IiFbOa6wHLI	
The Wild and the Wonderful		135
Empty Canvas	https://youtube.com/shorts/EO0C8tQT3W4	

Part Seven: 110 Emotions to Make You Crazy or Bring New Life 137

The Gift of Light		143
Twilight Shadows	https://youtube.com/shorts/-r2xGK4xf9s	
After The Storm		145
Breath Spaces	https://youtube.com/shorts/a2lNAQrseic	
Aloha		147
Star Stories	https://youtube.com/shorts/BYaEHcVYOZA	
Imagine		149
Bone Memory	https://www.youtube.com/shorts/Lt6EW4MbSis	
SOAR		151
New Songs Rising	https://youtube.com/shorts/jTXyhNnJSuk	
Forest on Fire		153
Path in Ruins	https://youtube.com/shorts/jimhR9tjm24	
Kake Walk		155
River Memories	https://youtube.com/shorts/slwfL2R5AB4	
Universal Whirlwind		157
Void Creation	https://youtube.com/shorts/QMdugb8A38k	

Part Eight: It's Your Turn 159
Heart Sutra 167
Sacred Between   https://youtube.com/shorts/FkeBsakjbNI
New Year's Day 169
Tangled Wisdom   https://www.youtube.com/shorts/UP4PYuF6pe0
Flock of Glow 171
Wilderness Between   https://youtube.com/shorts/rHZjl9DFXKw
Australia 173
Wound Watersheds   https://www.youtube.com/shorts/mNYeb3BnVkY
Mount Lily Lemmon No. 1 175
Sacred Text   https://www.youtube.com/shorts/SbG5RQ0T498
Mount Lily Lemmon No.2 177
Language of Soil   https://www.youtube.com/shorts/xnlCOvsmqeM
Ukraine Glows Forever 179
Wound Doorways   https://youtube.com/shorts/hqvaLNG8hM0
Free Will 181
Lost Rivers   https://youtube.com/shorts/C1B56PaucY8
Haunted Pumpkin 183
Unraveling Text   https://youtube.com/shorts/3y4Rp-57yOk
Let Something Wild Loose 185
Empty Cradle   https://youtube.com/shorts/RqDdwW6xOmY
Shadow Glow Guardian 187
Dancing With Our Shadows   https://youtube.com/shorts/mixIXXKZak0
The Endless Summer 189
Ocean's Whisper   https://youtube.com/shorts/CreGojWNu3w

Part Nine: Sharing Our Glow: A Journey into Emotional Wilderness 191
The Weeping St. Francis 199
Lost Compass
The Whitestone Dreamporium Glow Gallery: Can you ever lose at dreaming? 201
Whitestone's Glow Paint Adventure 203
Time Spiral 205
Whitestone's WanderLust Map   https://youtube.com/shorts/sErZsxmynaE
Rewild Your Soul, Reclaim Your Life, Create Something Original 206
It Takes a Village to Raise an Artist 209
Whitestone's Resources That Help You Heal, Feel, and Create 211
Whitestone's The Art of Letting Go: Wear The Glow 213
Integrate Everything Within   https://youtube.com/shorts/ZJ6hNtxbBl0 215

Most photos in this book were taken by the author on his journey of descent and return from 2010-2025.

"This book—each brushstroke of paint, word, and video vibrating with intention, each color born from the deepest chambers of my soul—is my LOVE offering to humanity, a sacred flame I've tended through my darkest nights so it might now illuminate yours."

—Jeffrey Bryan Grubert, Whitestone

***Revelation 2:17 (NRSV):** "Let anyone who has an ear listen to what the Spirit is saying to the churches. To everyone who conquers, I will give some of the hidden manna, and I will give a white stone, and on the white stone is written a new name that no one knows except the one who receives it."*

In today's language, we might say this truth is about finding "your" authentic self after working through life's difficulties—an identity so personal and true that only you can fully understand it, yet it becomes the foundation from which you live your most meaningful life.

(This is why I say, "'Cause WE all be stones!")

Whitestone's The Art of Letting Go To Glow

Wild Wanderings, Feel Everything, Create Something Beautiful

When I first considered how to write a book about transforming emotional intelligence into a more creative and meaningful life, I realized that traditional language would never capture what my glow art would have to say about the process. I realized that each vibrant canvas is more than glow art—each is a visual testament to a 40-year journey of inner awakening. A journey that started with avoiding my feelings to a journey of allowing them to have a voice and an impact that I could not express any other way.

Painting glow art emerged as my primary spiritual practice—a picture language that translates emotional intelligence into creative expression. These paintings don't hide my mistakes; they honor them. They document not a victim's story but a surrender story, where each setback became a stepping stone toward something more authentic. As I pondered the book, I realized that everything emerging from the art was coming from the practice of painting. The books, the creative one-on-one coaching, video courses, poetry, and wilderness intensives. I am honoring the gifts I've received from the art by writing the book and hoping they will inspire you to start trusting your own creative desires.

My journey unfolded alongside building a home entertainment business and raising three beautiful daughters with my music-loving wife. I deliberately carved out time not only for family but for my own spiritual growth, never suspecting how these parallel paths would eventually converge.

The spiritual doors kept opening as I walked through them—first into AA at 26, then a conversion to Catholicism at 27, followed by discovering Fr. Richard Rohr's Center for Action and Contemplation. But it was in Bill Plotkin's wilderness-based healing community where everything intensified and finally cohered. There, tracking my wild "monkey mind" alongside learning the soul-centric wheel of human development, I discovered the transformative power of wilderness immersion.

Through years of retreats and vision fasts, I found something both simple and profound: nature isn't just a beautiful backdrop—it's an active participant in our transformation. Each time I ventured into mountains, deserts, and canyons, I employed a gentle trick against my resistant mind. While my thoughts would scream warnings about wasted time and potential dangers, something remarkable happened once I arrived. My analytical mind would gradually surrender its grip, allowing my feelings to emerge as trusted guides.

The name "Whitestone" first came to me during a men's rites of passage at Ghost Ranch in Abiquiu, New Mexico, where I sat in cool red sands surrounded by the vibrant palette of desert life. I carried this name secretly for 19 years, receiving deeper insights about its meaning with each return to the wilderness. Mentors appeared precisely when needed, offering guidance that eventually led to the emergence of Whitestone The Glow Artist, creating paintings in three dimensions.

This journey itself became an ongoing work of art—a daily practice of surrendering to the unknown, meeting mystery with open arms, and following guidance that often appeared in unexpected forms. The wisdom stones I've gathered along this path are what I most want to share with you. Why? 'Cause we all be stones!

I created this book as more than a showcase for my glow art—I envisioned it as a practical resource to help others transform their emotional intelligence into a more creative life. One question I like to ask when people see my art is, "How does it make you feel?" My deepest hope is that it inspires people to discover how nature can shift consciousness, deepen emotional capacity, and lead them toward authentic creative expression.

Yet I must acknowledge a truth: to benefit from these pages requires a certain desperation—a hunger for something more than what conventional living offers, a willingness to fall in love with the protective yet limiting parts of the psyche, and a desire to embrace the four facets of wholeness outlined in Bill Plotkin's *Wind Mind: A Field Guide to the Human Psyche*.

Any transformational process requires facing the paradox of mind. Without awareness or inner work, our minds become adversaries, but when we embrace our inner lives, these same minds transform into our greatest allies. This requires effort—but effort that eventually feels like play, becoming a journey a person can welcome rather than endure.

The paintings you'll find in these pages aren't simply works I created—they're markers of moments when I stopped resisting what is and allowed something greater to flow through me. Each one represents a time when letting go led to an unexpected glow, when surrender became not defeat but enlightenment.

I hope my art conveys essential playfulness and that the colors flowing through these works deliver their ultimate message: no matter how dark it gets, there is always more light. My invitation is that you'll begin your own relationship with the natural world, learn the art of wild wandering, practice feeling everything without judgment, and start creating something unique, original, and beautifully yours.

Above all, I hope to ignite the fire of human imagination—something our world needs now more than ever. May this book serve as both inspiration and practical guide, offering stones of wisdom I've collected on my own path. After all, I found one of the most beautiful stones to be the whitestone because it brings contrast to thousands of others. That is why I glue a real whitestone on every painting. May this process of transforming emotional intelligence into creative expression bring peace to all who seek it, ultimately contributing to peace on earth as swiftly as possible.

PART ONE

You Are an Artist: A Human Fact

"The aim of art is to represent not the outward appearance of things, but their inward significance." —Aristotle

I remember when the idea hit me like a lightning bolt: I wasn't just a recovering addict—I was an artist who had temporarily lost access to my authentic creative expression.

Let me be clear—when I say, *"You are an artist,"* I'm not handing out a feel-good participation trophy. I'm pointing to a fundamental truth about being human that took me decades to fully grasp. This isn't motivational fluff; it's a biological fact.

Think about it. You were creating before you could speak—finger paintings, sandcastles, imaginary worlds. Nobody taught you how. The creative impulse is hardwired into our DNA, as natural as breathing. But somewhere along the way, many of us bought into the lie that creativity belongs to a special class of "talented" people—not ordinary folks like us.

I remember winning a writing award at Purdue University in 1980 for the best short short story in the English Department. I wasn't even an English major—I was studying radio/TV production. I had simply responded to a call for submissions, and somehow, I won.

What shocked me even more than winning was seeing my father walk into the ceremony. He had driven 200 miles to watch me receive a $50 gift certificate to the campus bookstore. This was the same man who rarely showed up for my sporting events or school functions throughout my childhood. Yet there he was, beaming with pride.

A year later, after I'd been fired from my job, he asked me over the phone what I wanted to do with my life.

"I want to be a writer," I told him, still glowing from that small moment of validation.

His response was immediate: *"There's no money in that."*

Four words. That's all it took to redirect the entire course of my life. I believed him completely, abandoning my writing dreams to pursue video production instead. Ironically, there wasn't much money in that either—at least not at first. The financial success I eventually achieved came from dedication, hard work, and yes, from the very writing skills I had nearly buried.

But that moment with my father wasn't really about him. He was simply passing down the same fear-based thinking he had inherited—a family lie about creativity and security that should have died with his generation, but instead found new life in me.

This is just one example of how cultural and familial conditioning can send us on detours that many never recover from. I look around and see so many people clinging to jobs they hate, relationships that drain them, and beliefs rooted in an addiction to safety. They've buried their creative desires so deeply into their psyche that those gifts may never see daylight.

When I speak about being an artist, I'm talking about breaking free from those conditioned responses, recognizing that the creative impulse within you is not a luxury or a hobby—it's the core of your humanity, desperately trying to express itself.

Let me be honest: nothing about this deconditioning process is easy. It often requires making difficult choices—letting go of comfortable habits that keep us from taking action. It might mean reimagining work situations or ending relationships that no longer align.

Yes, it's painful to make these shifts. But I can promise you from experience—it's far more painful to reach the end of your life having never expressed what was truly inside you. The pain of regret is sharper than the pain of growth.

At 26, I had to face the biggest challenge of my life. Admitting I was an alcoholic and a drug addict was the worst—and best—thing I ever did. That truth opened the door to every other transformation that followed. Trusting a process of failure and forgiveness became the bedrock of my sobriety.

Honestly, I've come to the end of myself a thousand times, going through the same surrender process I went through with substances. After all, money, property, and prestige can become addictions too—sometimes even more dangerous than the booze itself. But I was blessed to discover that living in recovery was an invitation to live in surrender, one day at a time.

And that's exactly where it gets interesting.

Recovery isn't just about stopping harmful behaviors—it's about reclaiming your role as the conscious artist of your life. Taking full responsibility means recognizing that I am participating in, and co-creating, my own reality. I am no longer a victim. I now see that life is happening *for* me, not *to* me.

When I finally got sober, I faced a terrifying blank canvas. Without my chemical shortcuts, how would I create meaning? How would I express the hurricane of emotions I'd been suppressing?

The breakthrough came when I embraced genuine creative practices by accepting an invitation to a wilderness healing program. Stepping into nature opened an expansive new landscape where I could finally *feel everything*. I surrendered to the powerful truth that my thinking was the real problem.

Though I'd heard countless times that how I think influences how I feel—and ultimately how I act—it wasn't until I immersed myself in the wild that I recognized the dysfunctional belief systems and cultural conditioning that had trapped me. I'd been chasing material success and personal achievement, convinced they would bring happiness.

For years, I understood intellectually that I couldn't *think* my way into better living—I needed to *act* first to change my thinking. And yes, that approach worked for a while. But it wasn't until I encountered Fr. Richard Rohr's teachings that I saw the bigger picture. I was still following the empty promises of the "American Dream." Despite all my success, I felt a persistent longing for something more authentic. Each achievement led to the same destination: emptiness and loneliness.

Then came the beautiful revelation: embracing that emptiness and loneliness could serve as a portal to the mysteries of the animate world. By practicing the art of letting go in nature, I journeyed into the darkness of my soul and found a magnificent realm where my imagination thrived.

In that safe convergence of mind and emotion, my internal chaos began to commune with the wild world around me. There, in my wild nature, I discovered wholeness. I realized that straight lines don't exist in the universe—everything belongs. The crooked path had been the perfect path all along.

Every recovering person knows the unique hell of feeling *everything* at once after years of feeling *nothing* at all. The blank canvas gave me somewhere to place those feelings: a rage-filled splatter painting, a grief-soaked poem, a sculpture made from broken things found on morning walks. Each act of creation became a declaration: *I am still here. I am still capable of transformation.*

My glow art emerged from deep within—a well of fear, sadness, and longing. And no matter how dark it got, more light would appear. In letting go, something magical always began to take shape. Time and again, I found that pushing through the fear and resistance led to something more beautiful. Joy emerged. I came to understand that death itself was just an illusion.

The paintings in this book are mystical, energetic, living testaments to what emerged from those dark explorations. My art motto became: *"Whitestone's Glow Art—With a Life of Its Own."* Their value lies in their testament. They want to be seen—just like you.

Emerging from the darkness brings forth the most glorious feeling of being truly alive.

What has come forth from my spiritual practice of glow painting is this: it's not about the paintings themselves—it's about the *glow* you and I carry within us. That light hides in the places we fear to go.

The good news from Whitestone? It's not only safe to go there—it's where you'll find your superpowers. Your magic. The kind that brings more light into the world.

And the Most Beautiful Part?

Once I started seeing myself as an artist, I realized that everything could be approached with creative intention. Making my bed became a daily installation piece—order emerging from chaos. Cooking became color theory and composition. Conversations became collaborative performances.

Recovery itself is the ultimate creative act—you're literally rebuilding a life, day by day, choice by choice. You're rewriting your story, reimagining your identity, redesigning your relationships.

If that's not art, I don't know what is.

This perspective shifts everything. Missing the mark—or relapse, as it's called in recovery—isn't failure. It's revision. It's a chance to learn something about your process. Difficult emotions aren't threats—they're raw materials waiting to be transformed. The past isn't a prison—it's just the first draft of a work still in progress.

When I embraced my identity as an artist, life stopped being about what I *couldn't* do and became about what I *could* create. The question changed from *"How do I just get through today without using?"* to *"What beauty might I bring into existence today?"*

This is why I believe so deeply in creative expression as a pathway to healing.

Journal writing becomes emotional archaeology.

Movement becomes embodied storytelling.

Music becomes the language of feelings that have no words.

Through these practices, we reclaim our power as creators rather than consumers, as active participants rather than passive victims.

So when I tell you *you are an artist*, I invite you to recognize what's always been true.

Your life is your primary canvas.

Your choices are your brushstrokes.

Your relationships are your collaborative works.

Your recovery is your masterpiece in progress.

And like any worthwhile art, it won't be perfect. It will have false starts, experimental phases, and sections you might paint over later. But it will be *authentically* yours—a creation no one else could possibly make.

This is *The Art of Letting Go to Glow*: releasing the expectation of perfection, surrendering the need for control, and allowing your natural creative light to shine through the cracks of your beautiful, broken, healing humanity.

This journey might speak to your unexplored wilderness.

When was the last time you let nature slow your pace and amplify your senses?

Consider spending an afternoon this week beside a stream or beneath a tree's canopy. Notice how your emotional landscape shifts in those spaces. Let the natural world's rhythms inspire your creative expression—perhaps through journaling, photography, or simply being present.

The wilderness isn't just *out there*—it's within you too. And it's waiting to teach you about your beautiful complexity.

Take one small step toward honoring that wild, creative force today. Your emotional life—and your artistic spirit—will thank you.

Note:

Throughout this book, I've included prompts—statements and questions to ponder, to wander with, to write about, to feel into—to help you spark your creative process. In the back of the book, you'll find a complete list of these prompts to use as a journaling guide. I hope you find them helpful.

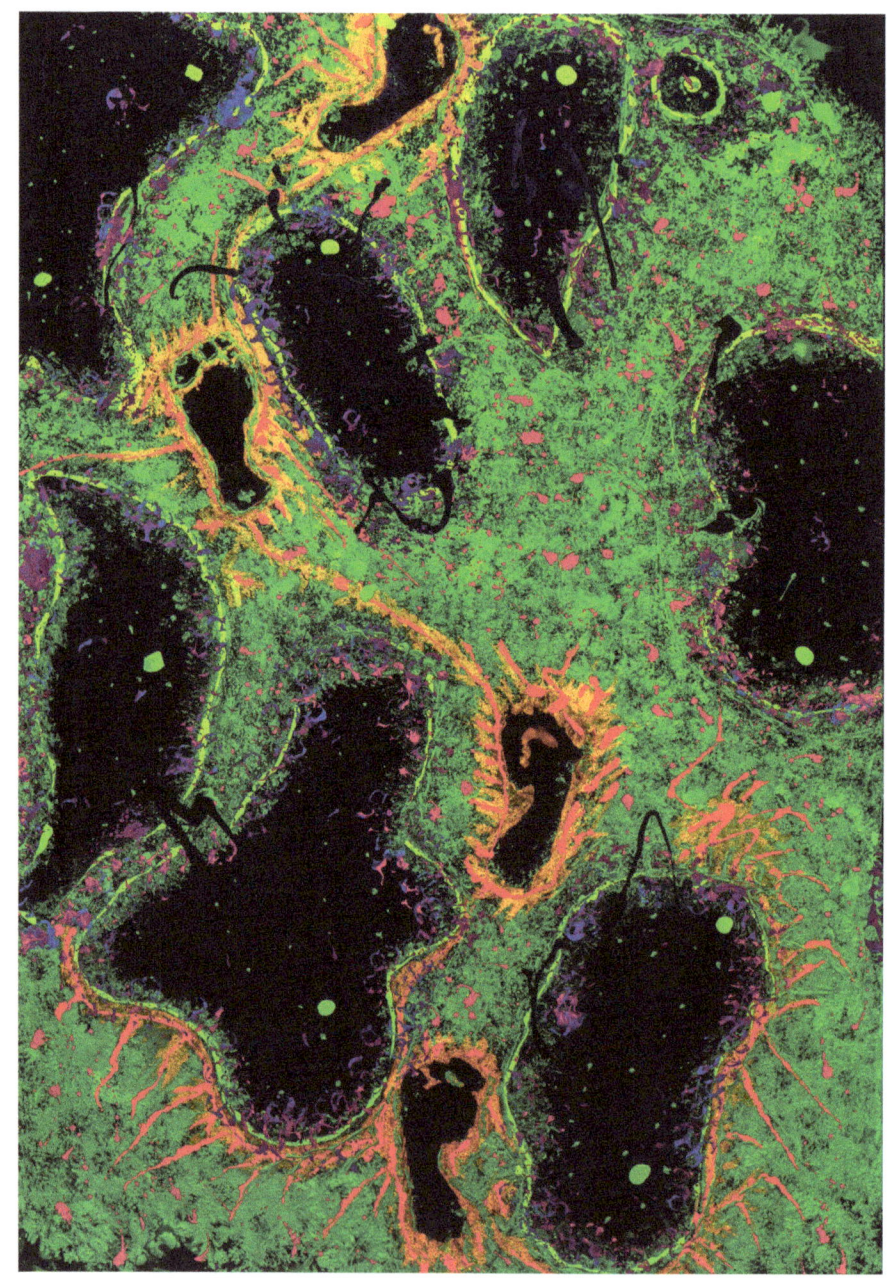

First Steps Into Aquarius

What do you see in the painting? What does it feel like to be stepping out of your comfort zone?

First Steps Into Aquarius

I found myself wading through the dark waters of consciousness when creating "First Steps into Aquarius." The fluorescent greens were planned—they emerged from visions of patches of glowing grass in the Northern California mountains where, on a sacred tea retreat, I was called from the darkness of my inner wilderness into the light of a fiery midnight moon. Each barefoot print that appeared as I walked across the canvas with mud stained feet became a sacred walk as I tried to imprint my memories of that sacred night, that step into the age of Aquarius. For added invisible effect, I spat brown tobacco on the foot imprints, embedding the ancient belief that tobacco—a sacred plant used for spiritual ceremony—carries the gift of healing.

The black voids became the vast universe that I was walking on—spaces that under the glow in the dark version would open up across the canvas, making way for the appearance of a constellation-type image of a bird and the words "Fly Ground" appearing. (Scan the QR code to see that glow version.) That beautiful evening in Northern California showed me how glowing grass reclaims abandoned places, how fungi transform decay into possibility. How my imagination could open up a unique depiction of an experience I will always remember. The most exciting fact about this work is that I had only a small vision that opened into a much larger one—a universal mysterious truth that brings joy to my life each day. I didn't just paint this piece—it forged new neural pathways through me as I collaborated in the dark with my muse and the mystery of the universe. The age of Aquarius will be forever here with me, my first steps into my creative authority and personal enlightenment. Scan the QR code to Fly Grounded in the dark.

Brushstroke Stars

Each brushstroke became a constellation mapping the geography of surrender and rebirth. Splashing stars across the dark open holes canvas, I noticed how each dot of color paint began to connect with others, forming patterns like constellations in the night sky. Ancient people used stars to navigate their journeys and tell their most important stories. My paintbrush did the same thing, mapping my invisible journey from giving up old dreams to discovering new ones. Scientists say when we look at stars, we see light that started traveling toward us long ago—some of it from stars already gone. When people saw my painting, they couldn't see all the false starts, the mistakes painted over, the moments I almost quit—but those invisible layers were part of the map too. Now when I paint, I think of each brushstroke as both a star in my sky-map and as light traveling outward that might reach someone else long after this moment has passed.

Glow West

Can you create something strange from a pinecone lying on the ground?

Glow West

I stumbled upon ""Glow Owl"" in a feverish fury of emotional excitement. Those twin pink circles came forth, glaring at me. in the face— I immediately fell in love with something mysterious beginning to appear. I mixed that particular shade of coral-pink on a whim, but once it covered the canvas, I understood it was the exact hue of that light that comes just before sunset breaks.

The owl emerged gradually, revealing itself through layers of intuition rather than conscious design. Those eyes—watching, knowing, seeing through my pretenses. I worked with pointed plastic- tip brushes that created streaks of colorful energy. This owl had wisdom coming straight from my imagination.

The verdant explosions of green—they came during a moment of surrender, when I stopped trying to control the outcome and, instead, became a conduit for something ancient and wild. I remember taking a deep breath of relief when the feathered wings took shape. The paint became my best friend as I turned on the black light to continue its birthing.

What began as a tirade of emotion transformed into a wild creature. I was happy to see him with a deep desire to be seen— like me. The owl"s body now holds all the tumultuous energy of what flight might feel like at twilight, that sacred moment when launching into the night might bring a new light to the world.

I never know what waits beneath the surface until I brave the journey downward, following glow paint into mystery, allowing myself to become lost so that something unexpected might find its way home through me. This Glow Owl is not only crying to be seen but looking for a final place to call home. Scan the QR Codes to see the UV pop. This is an early work with not much glow emerging.

Animate Riddles

The animate world spoke in riddles until I abandoned translation. The trees whispered secrets in rustling tongues while stones told silent stories through patient presence. I tried to write down what they meant, to capture their wisdom in my notebook with careful letters. But nature's language refused these tidy boxes. Only when I closed my dictionary and opened my heart did the mountain's riddle unfold within me. The owl's question mark flight at dusk wasn't meant for my mind to solve but for my soul to witness. Now I sit with a creek-song and wind-poem without trying to turn them into human words. Some truths can only be known by letting them flow through you unchanged, like light through clear water, like breath through open lungs—riddles whose answers live in experience rather than explanation.

River Tree

Can you see the paradox that is you, that is everything enfolding? Can you let go of your first thought, impression, or judgement and just go with the flow?

River Tree

The blank canvas was screaming for my passion. Passion and flow are always part of the work—that liminal space where intention gathers like spring rain before the first rivulet breaks through parched earth. As the tree emerged, so did the river, two as one, just like everywhere in nature. A match made in heaven to keep life possible for all.

When it finally came, I painted in a fevered state. Those aquamarine currents that surge around the central trunk flowed directly from something untamed in me—grief I'd been carrying since last autumn when I stood beside that ancient cottonwood at the river bend, watching its bark reflect golden light while water murmured secrets at its roots.

The central column emerged, not as I planned but as it needed to be—scorched and scarred, yet vibrant with hidden life. I worked vertically, letting paint cascade downward like watershed memories, each droplet finding its own path according to laws beyond my control. I was excited when I turned the light off to see that purple emerged glowing, and the contrasting colors and brushstroke motions made this work pop off the page in black light.

This piece taught me how creation mimics the silent wisdom of nature: force against resistance creates beautiful deviation. What flows needs boundaries to find its form. What grows needs resistance to discover its strength. I didn't just paint a river tree—I became the riverbed, learning to hold both current and reflection, motion and stillness, a vessel for passage and a witness to what remains. I was so blessed to take this one home and let the glow of it fill my living room for over three months until a new, created piece took its place.

Grief River

My grief became a river, carving new channels through the bedrock of who I thought I was. After my father died, my sadness flowed like water—sometimes a gentle stream, sometimes a raging flood. I noticed how the creek behind our house creates paths through solid rock, not by forcing but by persistent flowing. Water finds the cracks, follows the natural weaknesses, and over time, it transforms the landscape. My grief worked the same way. It found the soft spots in my heart, the questions about life and death I'd ignored, and gradually carved new pathways for my thoughts and feelings. Scientists say the Grand Canyon was made by water patiently cutting through rock over millions of years. My sadness similarly carved beautiful new depths in me. Though painful, this reshaping allowed new underground springs to bubble up—compassion, gratitude, wonder—creating fertile riverside places inside me where new understanding could grow.

Glow Turtles

How do you feel gazing into the vast blue ocean at dawn? Can you imagine how the sea shows up in your mood in the morning?

Glow Turtles

The Glow Turtles came forth after swimming at Poipu Beach in Kauai in late summer. The aqua and teal background washed across my canvas like an underwater dream, a memory of that tide pool where I encountered the sweet little head popping up next to me. I stood in the warm ocean water, watching the secret movements of the tiny creatures navigating their liquid world.

The turtles emerged—unplanned—as if they'd been waiting beneath the surface of my consciousness all along. I found myself embedding those little luminous friends—each one a moment of clarity breaking through turbulent emotional waters. The circular shell patterns formed under my hands like ripples of thought expanding outward, connecting experiences I hadn't realized were part of the same journey.

The layers of paint on the original popped when I switched on the black light while painting. When the lights turned out, I was thrilled to see how they appeared connected with a seaweed-type connection. Don't forget to scan the QR code to see this one come alive.

I signed it "Whitestone," not because I created these beings, but because I was merely present for their arrival. The glow-in-the-dark surprise felt more honest than my name—acknowledging that my best work happened in those surrendered moments when I stepped aside and allowed something more ancient to speak through pigment and gesture.

The turtles remind me that our slowest, most deliberate movements often carry us to our most necessary destinations. Their patient journey across my canvas taught me to trust the gradual unfolding of creative intuition—each brushstroke a small act of faith in the direction of mystery.

Breath Rhythm

Between breath and silence, I found the rhythm of authentic creation. Watching waves rise and fall along the shore, I noticed how the ocean breathed—surging forward, pulling back, pausing briefly before beginning again. All nature follows this pattern: inhale, exhale, rest. Flowers open and close. Seasons push forward, then retreat. Even the stars pulse with light that brightens and dims. I tried copying this rhythm when making things—working intensely, stepping back, and then allowing quiet space before starting again. My art changed completely! It started feeling less forced, more like something growing naturally. Real creativity, I learned, needs that empty pause between efforts—just like music needs the spaces between notes to become a song. Now I trust the gaps and silences as much as the active parts. True creation happens, not just in the doing but in the breathing rhythm of effort and surrender.

Have Fun

How do you feel about doing something you don't think you can do?

Have Fun

I could feel it inside me, some electric joy, demanding expression the morning I started "Have Fun." I'd been so serious for months, wrestling with heavy themes that left me drained, hollow. When I flipped on the black light, that purple background exploded from the plain white canvas of the original. Make sure to click the QR code to see how bland the original looks and watch something explosive show up with the lights turned off. I believe it came from a place of pure rebellion, a refusal to continue the solemnity. The purple was like a bruised sky before a storm breaks. The gold fragments appeared accidentally as well. This painting is one of my first breakthrough works. I laughed out loud when I saw what I created and I thought, "How much fun."

So the name came before the painting finished. "Have Fun"—both directive and permissive—words I needed to hear after months of taking everything so seriously. The green forms emerged from somewhere beyond conscious decision, dizzy with the pure kinetic thrill of momentum. I found myself returning to this canvas with a liberation I'd forgotten, each session less about making and more about becoming, less about control and more about conversation, with something wild and wise already waiting within the colors.

This painting taught me that sometimes the most serious artistic truth reveals itself through laughter, through surrender to delight—that fun isn't frivolous but foundational, not separate from the creative journey but essential to its deepest currents.

Color Psalm

Each color emerged as a psalm singing the wilderness journey through which I had wandered home. Mixing paints one afternoon, I noticed how each color seemed to carry its own emotion and story—cobalt blue whispered about deep water I'd swum through, burnt sienna spoke of earth that had supported me, crimson recalled both bloodshed and sunset beauty. Without planning it, those colors began arranging themselves into a visual song of my journey through hard times back to myself. Many cultures and systems associate colors with specific meanings or energies—chakra systems, religious art, cultural ceremonies. The Navajo associate black with north and blue with south in their sacred sand paintings that tell creation stories. When I stopped thinking of colors as just decorative choices and started listening to their deeper voices, my paintings became truthful prayers—each hue singing its part in the larger chorus of my life story. Now I select colors, not just for how they look but for what they're trying to say—letting cadmium yellow proclaim joy's return, allowing indigo to chant about night journeys, permitting green to whisper resurrection psalms as old as spring itself.

The Solar Life

Did you know that 100 trillion neutrinos pass completely harmlessly through your body every second? Google it!

The Solar Life

I began "The Solar Life" during the end of a successful career in residential solar sales. The luminous yellow emerged, not as color but as defiance, a refusal to surrender to the emotional eclipse caused by an ever-changing industry and the local electric companies' relentless attack on people's right to create their own power.

The central face formed itself while I worked with textured medium, appearing suddenly in the thick paste like an ancient petroglyph revealing itself through centuries of stone. I gasped when I saw it—this sun consciousness watching me as intently as I watched it. The relationship between observer and observed dissolved in that moment; I wasn't creating the sun so much as uncovering its presence already within me. What started as a serious thought became a reckless wandering into saving face.

This painting has a ridiculous amount of yellow glow paint that arrived by mistake. I simply dropped a gallon of paint on the floor, and to avoid its waste, I quickly poured as much as I could on top of the oval wood I glued to the canvas. From there, I added the dials and a happy face in the middle to show the sense of humor that arose while videotaping in the studio. Scan the QR code to see how the painting changes with light, to see how it glows and to watch a couple of short movies I made while painting. This painting taught me that creation doesn't always begin with vision but sometimes with saving face—the desperate need to externalize internal frustration too intense to contain. "The Solar Life" isn't just depicted in this piece; it became a tribute to a career that was vanishing before my eyes. Long live the solar life.

Filtering Light

My art began to glow when I stopped filtering light through the prism of expectation. Holding a glass prism to the window, I watched it break sunlight into all the colors hidden inside. But when I covered part of the prism, expecting only blue or red, I blocked the rainbow's full beauty. My art was like this too. When I tried forcing my paintings to match the picture in my head, they came out stiff and dull. But the day I just played with colors with no plan—the day my dog knocked over my water cup and I decided to let the spill become part of the picture—something magical happened. The painting began to glow with colors I hadn't even mixed on purpose! Nature doesn't filter sunlight or decide which flowers should grow where—it allows life to emerge in surprising ways. When I finally took my hands off the controls and stopped judging every brushstroke, my artwork began breathing with its own light. Now when I create, I whisper to myself, "Let the light come through unchanged," allowing the full spectrum of what wants to emerge instead of just the colors I think should be there.

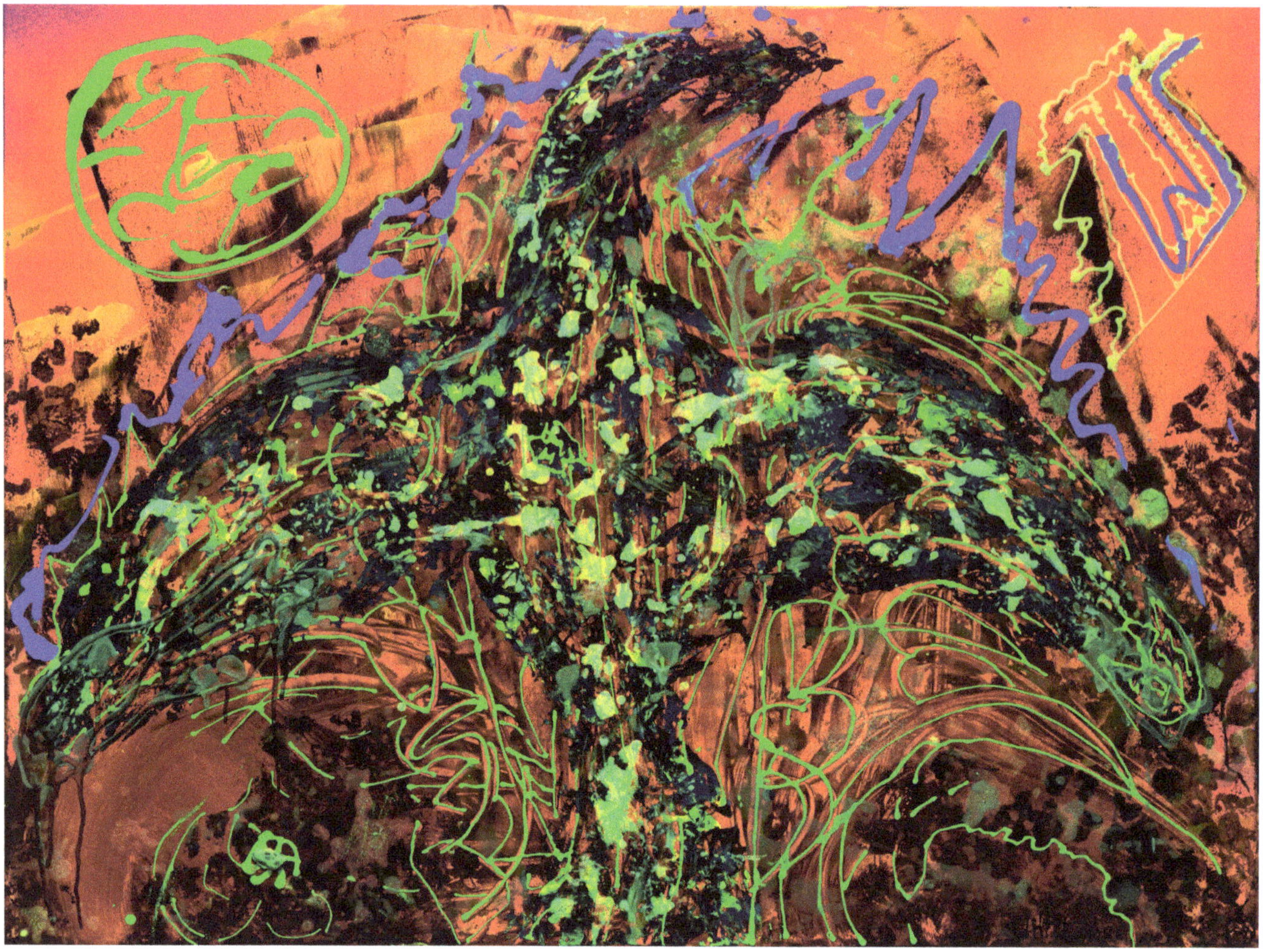

Emergence

What's lying dormant in your soul?

Emergence

I painted "Emergence" during a fevered dream of creativity that arrived unexpectedly after months of drought. That volcanic background wasn't planned—it erupted from some molten core of feeling I'd been suppressing beneath layers of intellectual restraint. When that fierce coral-red spread across my canvas, something primitive awakened in me, demanding expression beyond language or reason.

The emerald patterns appeared as if transmitted from another consciousness entirely. I remember standing before the canvas at 3:00 a.m., fluorescent paint dripping from my fingertips, watching those green tendrils reach and spiral like bioluminescent creatures rising from oceanic depths.

The mountain form emerged not through planning but recognition—suddenly, I saw it had been there all along, waiting to be acknowledged. When I added those final green highlights, what emerged was the form of an eagle disguised as a mountain. The painting wasn't just showing emergence—it was enacting it within me, reconfiguring my relationship to the creative force itself. Click the QR code to see how it emerges with the change of light.

Threshold Canvas

The canvas taught me that boundaries are not prisons but thresholds where meaning concentrates its essence. Staring at the wooden frame of my canvas, I used to feel trapped by its edges. Why couldn't my painting go on forever, like the view from the hilltop? But watching a family of rabbits at the forest edge one evening changed my understanding. They didn't stay deep in the protective trees, nor did they hop completely into the open meadow. Instead, they gathered at the boundary between, where they could access both safety and freedom, forest foods and meadow grasses. Scientists call these "edge habitats," where different ecosystems meet, and they're usually the richest places with the most diverse plants and animals. My limited canvas suddenly seemed less like a prison and more like a special meeting place where different worlds could touch, where my inner life could meet the outer world, where imagination could meet reality. The frame didn't restrict my expression; it created a focused doorway where meaning could become more concentrated and powerful. Now I see all boundaries—in art and life—not as walls but as thresholds where magic happens in the meeting of different worlds.

PART TWO

The Wanderer or Escapist - Unearthing the Gifts of Emotion

"When I draw, I breathe differently. When I paint, my breath follows the rhythms of the colors." —Vincent Van Gogh

Do You Know the Difference Between a Wander and an Escape?

This question hit me like a cosmic punchline at age 52, standing in the wilderness of Colorado with depth psychologist Bill Plotkin. I'd shown up to his "soul initiation" program thinking I was pretty self-aware. Spoiler alert: I wasn't.

Here's the raw truth—I wasn't a wanderer curiously exploring life's landscape. I was running like my pants were on fire, leaving scorched earth behind me. My business of 30 years was crumbling, my anger exploded like popcorn in a microwave, and I was absolutely exhausted from the marathon of pretending everything was fine.

I've learned something funny about emotions. We often treat our feelings like unwelcome houseguests, as if joy might raid the fridge or grief might put its muddy boots on our white couch. I spent decades perfecting this dance of avoidance myself.

Let me paint you the picture of my emotional education growing up: Mom was a rageaholic conducting symphonies of chaos, Dad was essentially emotional furniture trying to become invisible, and little me was taking mental notes thinking, "Well, I'll definitely never be like THAT."

So I did what any reasonable person would do—I ran. By 16, alcohol became my emotional GPS. By 19, cannabis was my daily meditation practice. Both promised relief but delivered handcuffs.

The comedy of errors climaxed when I got fired at 23 for lying to my employer—clocking in, pretending to visit clients, then hotboxing my car while driving aimlessly around town. Not exactly "Employee of the Month" material.

That afternoon on Laguna Beach, rock bottom had a skylight. My prayer wasn't exactly poetry: "Dear God, if you're there, I'm a total loser. The only thing I'm good at is smoking pot. I'm a drug addict." I bargained with the universe for a business opportunity, promising sobriety in return.

Looking back, 40 years later, I see that conversation as my first authentic emotional moment—scared, honest, no filters. But man, did I take the scenic route to emotional intelligence after that! The road to actually feeling my feelings was longer than necessary.

Here's what I've learned about embracing emotions as gifts rather than threats:

First, emotions are basically weather forecasts for your inner world. When I finally stopped running from anger, I discovered it was just trying to tell me, "Hey buddy, someone's crossing your boundaries!" When I sat with sadness instead of numbing it, it whispered, "This matters to you deeply."

Second, emotions are like those friends who tell you when you have spinach in your teeth—uncomfortable but incredibly useful. My anxiety, which I'd tried to suffocate with substances, was actually my intuition's alarm system trying to protect me.

Third—and this is where the magic happens—when you stop escaping your emotions, they transform from prison guards into creative collaborators. All that energy I spent running, I redirected into actual creation. The depth of feeling I avoided became the well I now draw from when making anything worthwhile.

And peace? It's not the absence of difficult emotions—it's having enough room inside yourself for all of them. It's like upgrading from a studio apartment to a mansion. Suddenly, there's space for joy *and* grief, anger *and* tenderness to coexist without anyone getting evicted.

I wish I could tell my younger self that emotions aren't the enemy—they're the map. Each feeling is a coordinate leading toward your authentic self. The difference between wandering and escaping isn't the terrain you're crossing—it's your relationship with the journey.

So here's my invitation, offered with a smile and the humility of someone who took the longest possible route. Stop running. Start wandering. Your emotions are weird, wonderful tour guides to places in yourself you never knew existed. And trust me—the view is worth it.

Finding Sacred Space in Nature

The wilderness taught me that intentional wandering creates sacred space for emotional honesty. When you step into nature with curiosity rather than desperate escape, something magical happens—the external landscape begins to mirror your internal one. The twisted oak becomes your stubborn resilience. The flowing stream embodies your grief. The soaring hawk reflects your highest vision.

Each time I venture into wild places, I bring questions instead of answers. I ask the mountains what strength really means. I inquire of the valleys what surrender might teach me. I wonder aloud to the wind what it knows about letting go. And remarkably, nature always responds—not with words, but with presence, with metaphor, with perfect synchronicities that speak directly to my heart.

Your emotional wilderness deserves this same gentle exploration. When you feel that familiar urge to escape—to numb out, check out, or run away—try something radical instead: wander toward the feeling. Get curious about its texture, its temperature, its message. Ask it why it's shown up in your life right now. Like tracking a shy forest animal, move slowly and with respect.

A Simple Practice: Emotional Wilderness Mapping

Find a natural space where you can be alone—a park, trail, garden, even a quiet spot under a single tree. Bring only a journal and writing utensil.

1. Begin by sitting quietly for five minutes, noticing your breath and the sensations in your body.
2. Ask yourself: "What emotion am I carrying today that needs to be seen?" Don't analyze, just notice what arises.
3. Stand up and begin walking slowly, with no destination in mind. Let your feet choose the path. Notice what in the landscape catches your attention—a certain tree, rock, patch of wildflowers, or play of light.
4. When something calls to you, stop and simply observe it. Ask yourself: "How is this natural element like the emotion I'm carrying?"
5. In your journal, create a dialogue between yourself and this natural element. What wisdom might it offer about your emotional state? What does this tree know about standing firm through storms? What does this water understand about flowing around obstacles?
6. Before leaving, find or create a small marker of your visit—arrange a few stones, tie grass into a small knot, or simply touch the earth with gratitude. This marks the spot where you honored rather than escaped your emotional truth.
7. Return to this practice regularly, tracking how your emotional landscape shifts and changes, just as the natural world does with the seasons.

Remember, the difference between wandering and escaping comes down to presence. Escaping means running from what is, while wandering means moving toward what might be. In nature, as in our emotional lives, the path forward often reveals itself only to those willing to be fully where they are.

Your creativity flourishes not despite your emotional complexity but because of it. The artist within you has been waiting for permission to use all the colors—not just the bright, pleasant ones society approves of, but the deep indigos of grief, the fiery reds of anger, the murky browns of confusion. The masterpiece of your life requires the full palette.

So step outside, feel the ground beneath your feet, and begin the sacred art of wandering—not to get away from yourself, but to finally, joyfully find your way home.

The Cosmic Christ

Do you know how to release your emotions to find a new path forward?

The Cosmic Christ

I approached "The Cosmic Christ" during a period of profound spiritual connection. That golden face emerged not from planning but from surrender—a moment when I stopped forcing meaning onto canvas and allowed something deeper to speak through my hands. The vibrant coral and green energy bursting from the pineal gland area wasn't something I consciously designed—it appeared as I allowed my brush to follow an inner knowing, revealing how our highest consciousness flows when we integrate all aspects of our psyche. Those swirling patterns show what happens when we stop compartmentalizing ourselves and allow both shadow and light to participate in our becoming.

The crimson elements forming the beard and clothing took shape during a moment of emotional catharsis. I found myself excited as they appeared, feeling as though I was witnessing transformation—the universal truth that there is always life after death, rebirth after dissolution—rather than creating it. This isn't just spiritual theory but the practical reality of our human condition—how endings continually birth beginnings when we're brave enough to release what no longer serves. Those white marks appeared last, like writing in a language I could feel but not translate, reminders that surrender to mystery always reveals something new arising from apparent emptiness.

The painting arose from a famous picture of the Tree of Life emerging from the pineal gland on an image of Christ. I was so moved by this image as it spoke directly to my personal experience with waking up and taking heed to the great mysteries of the mind itself. Click the QR codes to see "The Cosmic Christ" come alive. I also taped the photo I found to the back of the original canvas art.

Death's New Face

Death wears the face of transformation when viewed through dewdropped eyes. I used to think dead leaves were just garbage on the ground, but one morning, I saw dew on a brown leaf. Each tiny water drop was like a magnifying glass showing me how the leaf was becoming soil. Death isn't just an ending—it's a change into something new. The caterpillar looks like it dies in the cocoon, but really it's becoming a butterfly. When my pet goldfish died and we buried it in the garden, Mom said it would help the flowers grow. Now I see death differently. It's like when the seasons change—things don't just disappear, they transform. Looking through dewdropped eyes helps me see that nothing truly ends; it just changes into a different kind of alive.

Peace & Love in the Bedroom

Do you embrace your sexuality as a free form of expression or do you lock yourself down for fear of judgment or shame?

Peace & Love in the Bedroom

I began "Peace & Love in the Bedroom," attempting to honor my bedroom by including a Whitestone glow painting inside the larger painting. The square is that glow painting hanging on the wall in my bedroom. From that idea emerged the bed and then the images of two young lovers I'd spent some time with in beautiful sexual encounters. I drew the white flag of surrender, acknowledging there is more to a relationship than a sexual encounter. Don't forget to scan the QR code to see this one glow.

As I continued allowing my imagination to run wild, I viewed the painting as a world of fantasy and isolation. After completion and allowing the black light and the glow versions to appear, I noticed the face of a clown, which reminded me how much fun it was to just let the paint create a unique piece of work. Strangely, I perceived this painting to be an invitation to people into the passion of our sexuality without judgement. I must say that I've enjoyed hearing what other people think, which has allowed me to accept that I really don't have to know or explain the meaning behind this unique piece of work.

This painting taught me that sometimes our deepest emotional truths can only find voice through visual paradox—contradiction made visible through color and form—when words would only diminish the complexity of what thrums beneath the surface of our seemingly ordinary desires for peace and love in our most private sanctuaries.

Canvas Mirror

The blank canvas revealed itself as a mirror reflecting the wilderness I had wandered through. Setting up my first real painting easel, the empty white canvas scared me. What if I ruined it? But looking closer at that blank space, I began seeing reflections of places I'd been—like the white sand beach where I'd collected shells, the snowy field where I'd made angels, the fog that hid the mountain until I climbed through it. Empty space wasn't empty at all but full of memories and feelings waiting to be recognized. Many artists say they don't create paintings but discover them already hiding in the canvas. After walking through hard times that felt like wilderness, I found those experiences appearing in my art without planning them. Colors I chose, shapes that emerged—they carried the map of where I'd been. Now, before starting a new painting, I sit quietly with the blank canvas, letting it mirror back to me the inner landscapes I've traveled, showing me what needs to become visible.

Free Yourself

Do you want to know yourself? Are you willing to trust that God doesn't make junk?

Free Yourself

I started painting "Free Yourself" during an intense determination to create a painting that would show the intensity by which I explored the animate world for over 10 years. I painted the words "Free Yourself" over a hundred times during a four-hour session with many different colors of glow paint. When I was finished, the figure of a bird in flight emerged, carrying me to an awareness that freeing myself was a 100 percent inside job. Scan the QR code to see the three dimensions of "Free Yourself."

In the lower left-hand corner the word, "Nooooo," is spelled out and tied to a magic mushroom, depicting that with the help of plant medicine and a qualified medicine worker, the journey can be intense and explosive, yet full of resistance along the way. This painting is about breaking through the resistance and looking deep within to fall more deeply in love with our demons and to acknowledge the loyal service they provided when we were young. If we are to grow up, we must do the inner work and free ourselves. No one will do this work for us.

The background emerged not as color but as a declaration—sunshine frequencies vibrating against my skin, demanding to be translated through my hands into visible revelation. I mixed yellows until they hummed with the exact pitch of liberation I'd been hearing in my dreams.

This work taught me that freedom isn't an abstract concept but a physical sensation, a specific frequency of being that can be accessed through color and form when intellectual pathways have become overgrown with doubt. The yellow field isn't just background but foreground—the luminous possibility that exists before, during, and after every mark we make, waiting patiently for us to recognize its presence—even in our darkest hours.

Earth Courage

In surrendering to Earth's embrace, I found the courage to be both mortal and infinite. Lying flat on sun-warmed rocks one summer afternoon, gravity pulled me down while light pulled me up. I felt caught between these forces—my body heavy with its temporary nature, my spirit expanding beyond skin. The rock beneath me was ancient, formed millions of years before humans existed. It would remain long after my body returned to soil. Yet the atoms making up both rock and me were equally old—born in stars that exploded before Earth formed. I realized I am both a passing visitor and permanent resident of this universe. Like the mayfly that lives just one day but carries genes from ancient ancestors, I am both fleeting breath and eternal matter. This double truth gives me strange courage: I need not fear my smallness or deny my vastness. In Earth's patient arms, I found bravery to be exactly what I am—a temporary shape of everlasting stuff.

Visualize Your Dreams

Pay attention to your dreams or you will surely suffer the loss of your imagination!

Visualize Your Dreams

I entered my darkroom studio with "Visualize Your Dreams" already burning inside me—not as an image but as a directive from spirit. The phosphorescent green background emerged under black light as if my subconscious had been waiting for this specific frequency to become visible. I remember mixing those glowing pigments with the end of a mop, excited to see how it would apply the paint to the canvas, feeling like I was transcribing some urgent message from a realm just beyond ordinary perception.

The painting kept transforming under the oscillating ultraviolet light—revealing hidden dimensions, then concealing them again, teaching me that dreams exist in perpetual flux, visible only when we adjust our perception to their particular vibration. No matter how wonderful the colors exploded under black light and in the dark, I noticed that the original appeared in a soft pink and white mix or gentle display. I thought the original looked boring, so I had to leave my judgement with the natural light and let it transform when the lights were turned off. Scan the QR code to see the soft original painting and how dramatically it changes with black light and in the dark. Since the directive from spirit, "Visualize Your Dreams," felt cliche at the time, I decided to let the words appear unorganized and free flowing using the "UR" instead of "Your" and placing a dragonfly to help invite the human imagination into the experience.

This painting reinforced the reality that visualization isn't merely picturing what we want—it's creating a permeable boundary where dream and waking life can commune, where intention meets the wild wisdom of uncertainty. I have come to love my visualization practice, especially during my daily meditation practice.

Descent Ascension

My descent became ascension when I stopped measuring distance traveled. Climbing down into the canyon, I worried about going too far, getting too low. But at the bottom, looking up at circling hawks, I realized something: direction depends on perspective. From the birds' view, my downward journey was movement toward center, not bottom. Indigenous wisdom teaches that going down into earth, into darkness, into difficulty, is often spiritual climbing. Like seeds that must fall and be buried before they can grow upward, my journey into hard emotions—sadness, anger, fear—wasn't failure but necessary planting. When I stopped judging my path by how "high" I appeared to others, I discovered the truth: sometimes we must descend to rise more authentically. Going down into my deepest self revealed stars reflected in underground pools I never would have found by always climbing upward. Now I trust the spiral that takes me both down and up simultaneously, knowing they're the same journey seen from different eyes.

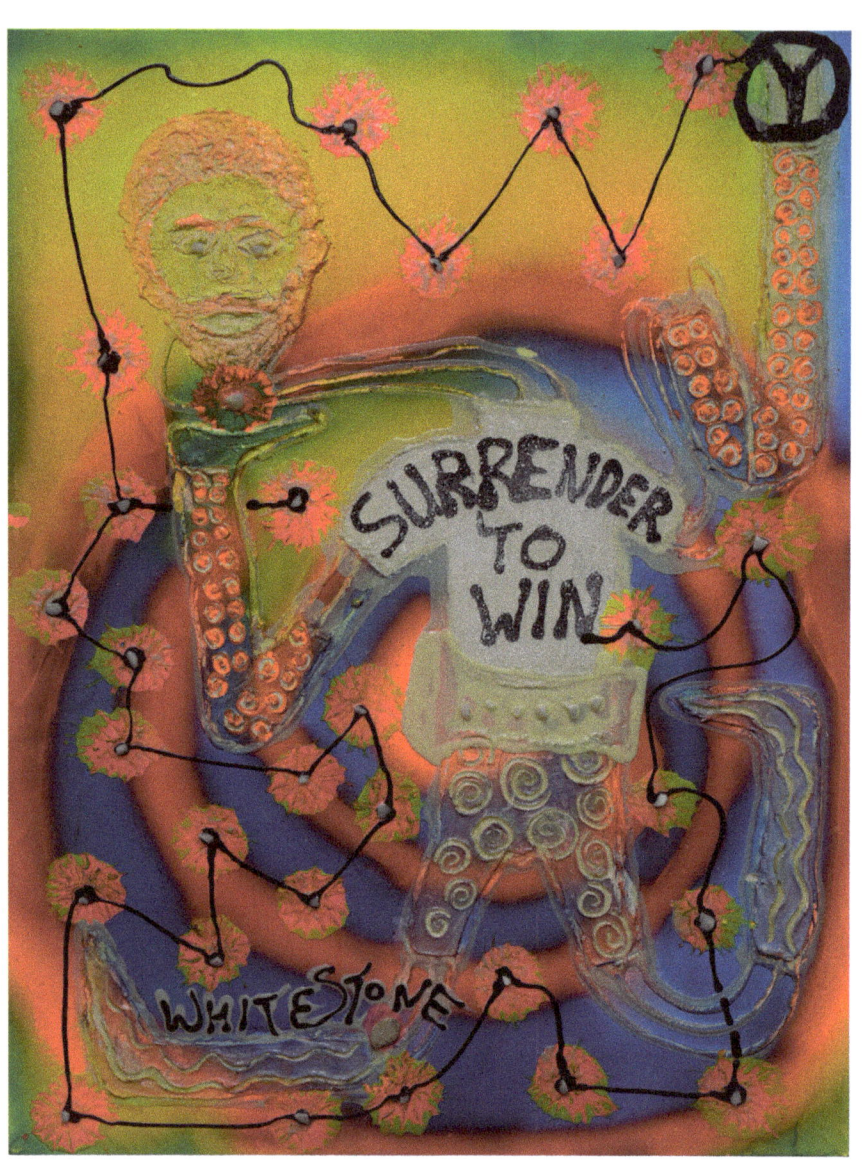

Surrender To Win

How do you feel when your life is falling apart?

Surrender To Win

I created "Surrender To Win" during a creative breakthrough that cracked open my artistic process. The rainbow target background erupted spontaneously, rejecting the safe, monochrome thinking that had limited me. What began as an intuitive circular design later revealed its deeper meaning—surrendering is precisely how we hit life's bullseye, teaching me to let go to glow.

The pink luminous nodes connected by black pathways emerged as I realized everything connects in surrender, inevitably leading to inner peace. Each glowing point maps a specific moment when complete release propelled me forward.

After creating the target, I began exploring the human form by first painting the head, then systematically dismembering arms and legs across the canvas. This fragmentation reflected my own painful transformation as an artist—parts separated yet still connected, capturing both the tearing apart and wholeness of profound change.

"SURRENDER TO WIN" appeared after days of wrestling with the painting. I wrote it half-blind, finally grasping the paradox: control imprisoned me while release empowered me.

Signing "WHITESTONE" felt right as usual on this work because stepping into this mythic artistic identity has deepened my understanding of surrender itself.

Pulse Connection

Earth's pulse became my own when I ceased counting the moments between loss and finding. Leaning against an ancient tree, hand pressed to its bark, I felt two heartbeats—the slow, steady rhythm of sap rising and falling, and my own quicker human pulse. At first they seemed separate, but as I quieted my thoughts, the rhythms began to synchronize. Indigenous wisdom teaches that Earth has its own heartbeat we can feel in drumming, waves, and seasonal cycles. When I stopped obsessively tracking my losses and gains, measuring my progress, I could feel this larger rhythm carrying me. Like joining a dance already in progress, I found my place in time's greater movement. The space between losing and finding wasn't empty waiting—it was part of the universal heartbeat: contract, expand, rest. Now, when I feel disconnected, I place my palm on stone, soil, or living wood, letting my pulse remember its connection to Earth's ancient drumming, the original music we all dance to.

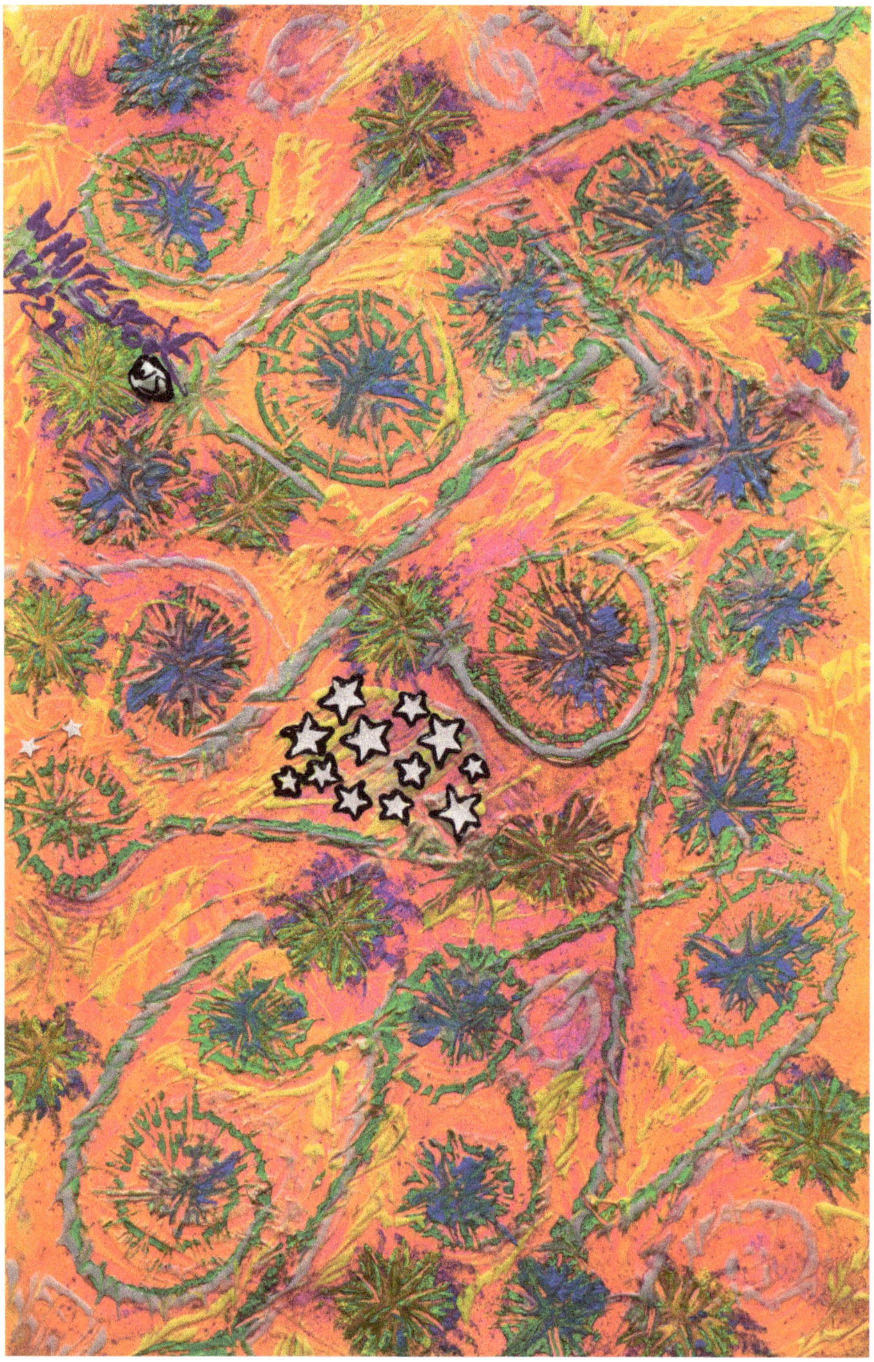

Simply Complicated

You are more than what you think.

Simply Complicated

I began "Simply Complicated" on a 30"x48" canvas during a period when paradox had become my closest companion. The vibrant coral background spilled across the surface almost rebelliously, defying my usual careful approach. I wanted to capture that precise feeling when contradiction becomes not a problem to solve but a mystery to celebrate.

Those circular starburst patterns emerged unplanned—each one a universe unto itself, yet part of the larger cosmic dance. As I painted, I thought about how we're constantly navigating opposing truths: how we're insignificant specks in an infinite universe yet contain infinite worlds within us, how the most profound understandings often come through the simplest observations.

The deliberate placement of those clustered stars in the center—a moment of structured pattern amid organic flow—mirrors how we seek organization within chaos, meaning within randomness. This dance between order and spontaneity is the heartbeat of both creation and community.

The interconnecting lines appeared as I reflected on how seemingly contradictory perspectives can be pathways to deeper understanding rather than barriers. In human relationships, embracing paradox creates space where differences don't divide but enrich.

This painting taught me that when we stop trying to resolve paradox and instead welcome its tensions, we create room for everything—every perspective, every creature, every possibility—to exist simultaneously in beautiful, complicated harmony. Scan the QR code and experience the simplicity of a complicated universe.

Holy Ground

Between the shattering and the becoming lies holy ground. When the clay pot fell off the porch and broke into pieces, I wanted to cry. But in the middle of the mess, a tiny seedling was growing where dirt had spilled out. That space between broken and new—that's special ground. Native people say certain lands are sacred, not to be walked on with shoes. I think the in-between places in our lives are like that too—holy ground that deserves respect. After my parents divorced, there was this strange time that wasn't the old life but wasn't the new life either. At first, it just felt broken, but then I realized it was also a beginning. Now I take off my emotional shoes—my expectations and judgments—when I'm in those between-times. They might look messy, but they're actually sacred places where magic can happen.

Fly Grounded

What are you doing to stay grounded before you act?

Fly Grounded

I painted "Fly Grounded" after receiving a divine directive in my studio—feeling simultaneously liberated and constrained, elevated yet anchored. The prismatic background emerged first, those sunset oranges bleeding into greens and purples like atmospheres shifting between different states of being. The bird arising as the central image was perfect for the reflection as even a newborn chick needs to fall to the ground before learning to fly.

The explosive luminous streaks that rose upward weren't planned but erupted from somewhere primal in me—a visceral need to transcend limitations while the black drips and splatters at the bottom pulled in the opposite direction, grounding the composition in gravity's honest truth.

Those electric blue letters announcing "FLY GROUNDED" appear in this black light version of the work—the paradox that had been haunting me finally finding its voice through color and form.

The chaotic black splashes across the bottom edge weren't mistakes but deliberate surrender to the fact that the earth holds all the wisdom, and we must embrace its wisdom in order to become our authentic self. These earthbound elements create tension with the ascending light, the necessary counterpoint that gives flight its meaning.

This piece taught me that our deepest power often emerges at the intersection of opposing forces—that being simultaneously rooted and soaring isn't contradiction but completion. Sometimes we must stay firmly planted to truly fly, must our embrace limitations to discover our most profound freedom.

Bare Wild

The wilderness stripped me bare until I recognized my own wild nature. When the rainstorm caught me far from home with no jacket, I was soaked to the skin. At first, I felt embarrassed and exposed. But as I sloshed through puddles with my hair plastered down, something changed. I felt the rain directly on my skin, not through clothes. I tasted it on my lips. I realized I wasn't so different from the dripping trees or the wet rabbits hiding under bushes. We were all just living things getting rained on together. The wilderness has a way of washing away all the fake stuff—like how we pretend to be "civilized" and different from animals. When I was completely soaked, with mud on my legs and leaves in my hair, I recognized something—I'm part of this wild world too. I've always been wild inside, just like the deer and the hawks.

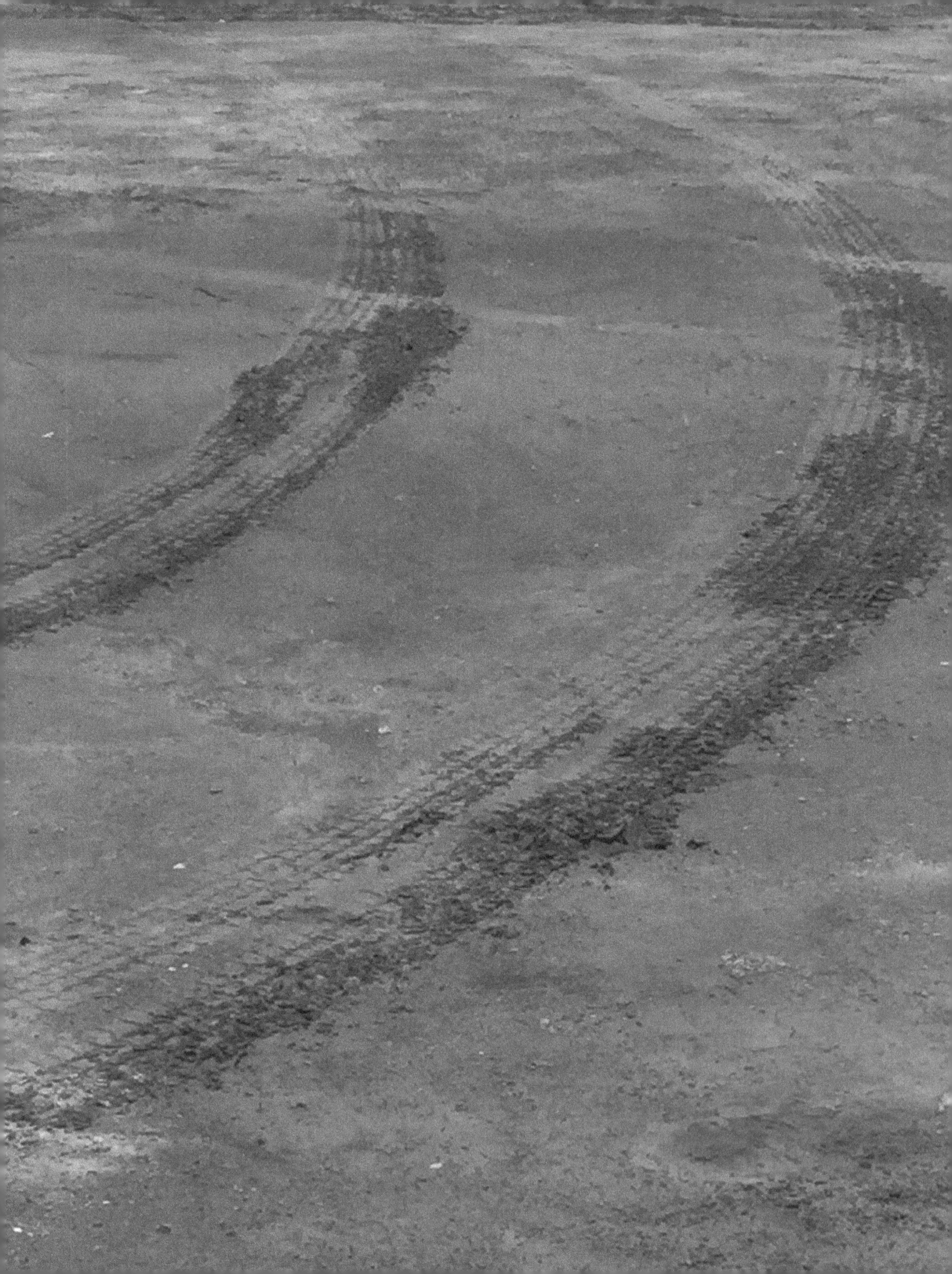

PART THREE

Waking up in the Prison of Your Mind

The Guest House

#

This being human is a guest house.
　　Every morning a new arrival.

#

A joy, a depression, a meanness,
　　some momentary awareness comes
　　as an unexpected visitor.

#

Welcome and entertain them all!
　　Even if they're a crowd of sorrows,
　　who violently sweep your house
　　empty of its furniture,
　　still, treat each guest honorably.
　　He may be clearing you out
　　for some new delight.

#

The dark thought, the shame, the malice,
　　meet them at the door laughing,
　　and invite them in.

#

Be grateful for whoever comes,
　　because each has been sent
　　as a guide from beyond.
　　—*Jellaludin Rumi*

The Dawn of Recognition

The first light comes not as brilliance but as shadow—a subtle darkening that paradoxically illuminates. You begin to see the bars that have always surrounded you, bars forged from thoughts hammered into shape over decades, polished by repetition until they gleam with the false luster of truth. This is the bewildering dawn of awareness: discovering you have never been awake.

Imagine a sleepwalker who, mid-stride through a familiar dream, feels the cool kiss of dew on bare feet. Something penetrates—a whisper from reality, a sensation that doesn't belong in the choreographed dance of unconsciousness. The sleepwalker doesn't immediately wake, but experiences that first disorienting question: *Am I dreaming?*

This is where liberation begins—not in full consciousness, but in the first doubt of your certainty.

The prison of the mind constructs itself so elegantly that we mistake its architecture for the natural world. We believe our thoughts are simply observations of reality rather than interpretations filtered through layers of conditioning, trauma, inherited beliefs, and protective mechanisms. We look out at life through windows clouded by fingerprints from everyone who ever touched our becoming—parents, teachers, friends, strangers, culture, media—and mistake this smudged perspective for clear vision.

The Circular Path of Imprisonment

Inside this prison, a well-worn path circles endlessly:

A thought arises: *"I'm not enough."*
This thought triggers emotions: *shame, anxiety, fear.*
The emotion drives actions: *withdrawal, overachievement, numbing.*
The action reinforces the thought: *"See? If I were enough, I wouldn't need to…"*

And so the cycle continues, a snake eternally consuming its tail, a wheel turning in deep ruts. This is the machinery of unconsciousness—thought creating emotion creating action creating thought—a perfect system of self-perpetuation that requires only your unawareness to function.

Most of us try to intervene at the level of emotion or action. We attempt to feel better without addressing the thought that spawned the feeling. We try to act differently while carrying the same emotional weather inside us. Like trimming the visible portion of weeds while leaving roots intact, these approaches offer temporary relief at best.

The breakthrough comes in recognizing the headwaters of this river: thinking itself.

The Moment of Reckoning

There is a sacred, terrible moment when you truly see the prison for what it is. When you understand that your thinking—this constant companion, this trusted advisor, this seemingly essential process—has been both architect and warden of your confinement. That your emotions, those apparent oracles of truth, are merely messengers carrying information created by your thoughts. That your actions, which you believed sprung from authentic desire, have been reactions to emotions triggered by thoughts that may have never been true.

This moment feels like vertigo, like the foundations beneath you are turning to sand. If you cannot trust your own mind to perceive reality accurately, what can you trust? If your emotions aren't reliable guides, what is? If your actions have been automatic responses rather than conscious choices, who has been living your life?

This is the threshold of awakening—confusing, disorienting, and utterly necessary.

The Birth of True Awareness

Awakening doesn't arrive fully formed. It emerges in fragments, in moments of clarity that punctuate long stretches of familiar unconsciousness. You might suddenly recognize a thought pattern while engaged in it, like catching your reflection in an unexpected mirror: *There I am, believing that story again.* You might feel an emotion arise and watch it with curiosity before being swept into its current: *Interesting—rejection still triggers this ancient fear.*

These moments lengthen gradually. The space between thought and emotion widens. The pause between emotion and action grows more accessible. In these widening gaps, choice becomes possible.

This is not about controlling thoughts or suppressing emotions—such efforts only fortify the prison walls. It's about developing the capacity to witness the inner landscape without immediately becoming it—to observe the weather systems of your mind passing through without believing they define you.

True freedom isn't the absence of difficult thoughts or challenging emotions. It's the spaciousness to experience them without compulsion—to feel everything without becoming enslaved by what you feel, to think without believing every thought that crosses your mental sky.

Four Liberations to Free Yourself

The journey from unconscious imprisonment to awakened choice requires practical pathways. Whitestone's Four Liberations offer tangible steps toward freedom:

1. The Liberation of Witness Consciousness

The mind cannot be both subject and object simultaneously. When thoughts arise, practice shifting from being the thinker to watching the thinking. This simple but profound movement—from "I am angry" to "I notice anger arising"—creates the first essential space of freedom.

Practice: The Thought Stream Meditation

Find a quiet place where you won't be disturbed. Sit comfortably and close your eyes. Imagine your thoughts as leaves floating on a stream. As each thought arises, mentally place it on a leaf and watch it float away. Don't try to stop thoughts from coming—simply observe them passing by without following them downstream. When you notice you've been carried away by a thought, gently return to watching the stream. Practice this for five minutes daily, gradually increasing the duration.

This practice strengthens your ability to differentiate between having thoughts and being had by them. Over time, you'll develop the capacity to observe your thinking patterns without automatic identification, creating space for conscious choice.

2. The Liberation of Cognitive Reframing

Our minds construct reality through interpretation. The same event can be perceived as catastrophic or challenging, depending on the frame we place around it. Learning to recognize and reshape these frames liberates us from the tyranny of singular perspective.

Practice: The Three Viewpoints Exercise

When facing a challenging situation, deliberately adopt three different perspectives:

- The Fearful Mind: What's the worst interpretation? What am I afraid this means?
- The Neutral Observer: What are the objective facts, separate from my interpretation?
- The Compassionate Sage: What might a wise, loving mentor see in this situation?

Write down each perspective, noting how each feels in your body. Notice which perspective you habitually default to, and practice intentionally shifting between them. This develops cognitive flexibility—the ability to view situations through multiple lenses rather than remaining trapped in a single, often distorted frame.

3. The Liberation of Embodied Wisdom

The body holds intelligence our analytical minds cannot access. While thoughts can spiral endlessly, the body always exists in present reality. Learning to listen to somatic wisdom provides an anchor outside the prison of mental constructs.

Practice: The Body Compass

Recall a situation when you felt deeply right and aligned with your truest self. Notice where and how this registered in your body—perhaps warmth in your chest, relaxation in your shoulders, or steadiness in your breathing. This is your body's "yes" signal.

Now, recall a situation that felt wrong or misaligned. Notice those different sensations—perhaps tightness in your throat, constriction in your stomach, or shallow breathing. This is your body's "no" signal.

Throughout each day, pause before making decisions and check your body compass. What is your somatic wisdom communicating? This practice bypasses the mind's habitual patterns, accessing deeper intelligence that often perceives truth more clearly than our thoughts.

4. The Liberation of Conscious Action

Ultimate freedom comes through doing—taking actions aligned with your deeper values rather than reactive behaviors driven by unconscious patterns. These actions gradually reshape your neural pathways, creating new possibilities for thinking and feeling.

Practice: The Pattern-Breaking Ritual

Identify one recurring situation where you habitually react in ways that don't serve your well-being. Perhaps you withdraw when criticized, overeat when anxious, or lose your temper when feeling vulnerable.

Design a specific, intentional action that contradicts this pattern. Make it simple and concrete: "When criticized, I will take three breaths before responding." "When anxious, I will walk for five minutes before deciding whether to eat." "When angry, I will place my hand on my heart before speaking."

Practice this alternative action consistently for 21 days, tracking your experience in a journal. Notice how different actions gradually create different thoughts and emotions, proving that the cycle can be interrupted and redirected through conscious choice.

The Landscape Beyond the Prison

As these practices take root, the prison walls begin to thin. You discover that awareness itself is not confined—it extends beyond the boundaries of conditioned thinking into vast, uncharted territories. In this expanded field, you find thoughts are simply weather patterns moving across the sky of consciousness, emotions are waves rising and falling in an endless ocean, and actions become creative expressions rather than compulsive reactions.

This awakening is not a destination but a continuous unfolding. There will still be days when the old prison feels solid, when you forget you're dreaming and believe the dream completely. But these periods grow shorter. The gaps of awareness widen. The space between stimulus and response expands into a realm of infinite possibility.

Waking up is realizing that reality is always more vast, more mysterious, and more fluid than your thinking can comprehend. The prison was never built of stone but of thought-forms mistaken for reality. And in the recognition of this truth lies the key that has always hung inside the cell, waiting for the moment when you finally see it.

Freedom is not the absence of thought but the spaciousness to let thinking happen without being defined by it. Not the absence of emotion but the capacity to feel everything without drowning. Not perfect action but conscious choice.

And it all begins with that first, humbling recognition: I have been asleep. I have been dreaming. I am ready to wake up.

Glow Butte Bird

How does nature mirror your connection to all living creatures?

Glow Butte Bird

I began "Glow Butte Bird," getting inspiration from the view of Thumb Butte just outside my studio door. What started as a portrait of this beautiful earth formation ended up an image of a bird rising from the wild Arizona Terrain. That rich terracotta background seemed perfect for the bright mood I was bringing to the canvas and the color of the dirt from the hikes I'd made many times. The textured ridges formed under my hands almost instinctively, my fingers remembering the sensation of touching ancient stone faces weathered by millennia of wind and rain. I worked with heavy medium, building topographical memory into the canvas, transforming my loneliness into something solid and enduring.

That central bird form emerged unexpectedly—I hadn't set out to create a creature, but as I carved into the thick paint with the end of my brush handle, something winged and powerful began to take shape. My grief about the environmental devastation I'd witnessed in formerly pristine places suddenly found expression through this resilient, elemental bird rising from earthen textures.

The white speckled areas appeared after I scattered wet glow paint, watching it draw pigment into crystalline patterns—mimicking the way salt deposits bloom across desert floors, how even harshness creates unexpected beauty when given time and space to interact with its surroundings. Make sure to scan the QR code to see the butte bird glow.

Soul Soil

My descent revealed how soul and soil share the same ancient spelling. Did you know "soul" and "soil" are almost the same word? I never noticed until I dug my hands deep into desert earth during the fall. As I let the cool earth run through my fingers, I felt a weird connection—like the soil understood something deep inside me. Both words come from old languages where they meant the same thing: the living essence that makes things grow. When I was at my lowest point, crying near a cottonwood tree, I pressed my face to the ground and felt dirt against my cheek. Something passed between us—the soil and my soul recognized each other. Both hold seeds of life waiting to sprout. Both get richer when broken down and mixed with new elements. When I touch the earth with respect, it's like I'm touching a part of myself I forgot was there.

Whirlwind

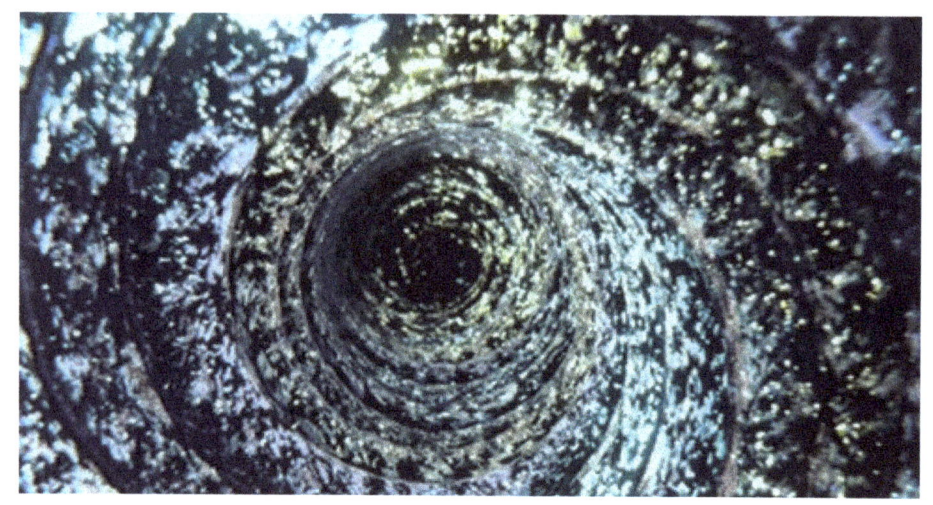

Can you open your imagination when something takes your breath away?

Whirlwind

Whirlwind arose from a pencil as I began dreaming about how the wind moves in swirls, never in a straight line. I was amazed that the bird image appeared as I began to apply paint to the stencil drawing I made on the canvas. Birds and wind are partners in flight. I would consider this one of my true masterpieces. I must report how sad I am that this painting was stolen and its whereabouts are still unknown. Or maybe it just blew away in a whirlwind? I would have put out a search party and offered a reward if I could have afforded it, but I still hope it will be returned to me soon. This is why I chose to include all three images of this special piece of work. I heard once that if one's artwork is stolen it's a true sign of its inherent value. Do you agree?

What began as an attempt to expel confusion transformed into a map of how transformation actually works—not through orderly progression but through spiraling cycles that continuously revisit and reinterpret what we thought we knew. The painting taught me that disorientation isn't failure but potentially the beginning of a new orientation, if I could just trust the process.

Breathing Art

My art began to breathe when I stopped demanding it speak in languages I already understood. Frustrated with my painting that didn't look "right," I nearly tore it up. But sitting with it silently, I noticed it was trying to say something in its own tongue—a language of shape and shadow I wasn't yet fluent in. Plants perform a kind of magic called respiration, taking in what we exhale and releasing what we need to breathe. True art works similarly—it breathes with its own rhythm, taking in our experience and transforming it into something that gives life back differently. Ancient cave paintings weren't trying to look "realistic" but to capture spirit and energy in their own powerful visual language. When I stopped forcing my art to use words I already knew and started listening to its native dialect, my paintings began to breathe—inhaling my experience, exhaling mystery. Now I approach my creative work with reverence for its separate aliveness, less like a master giving orders and more like a friend learning a beautiful foreign language.

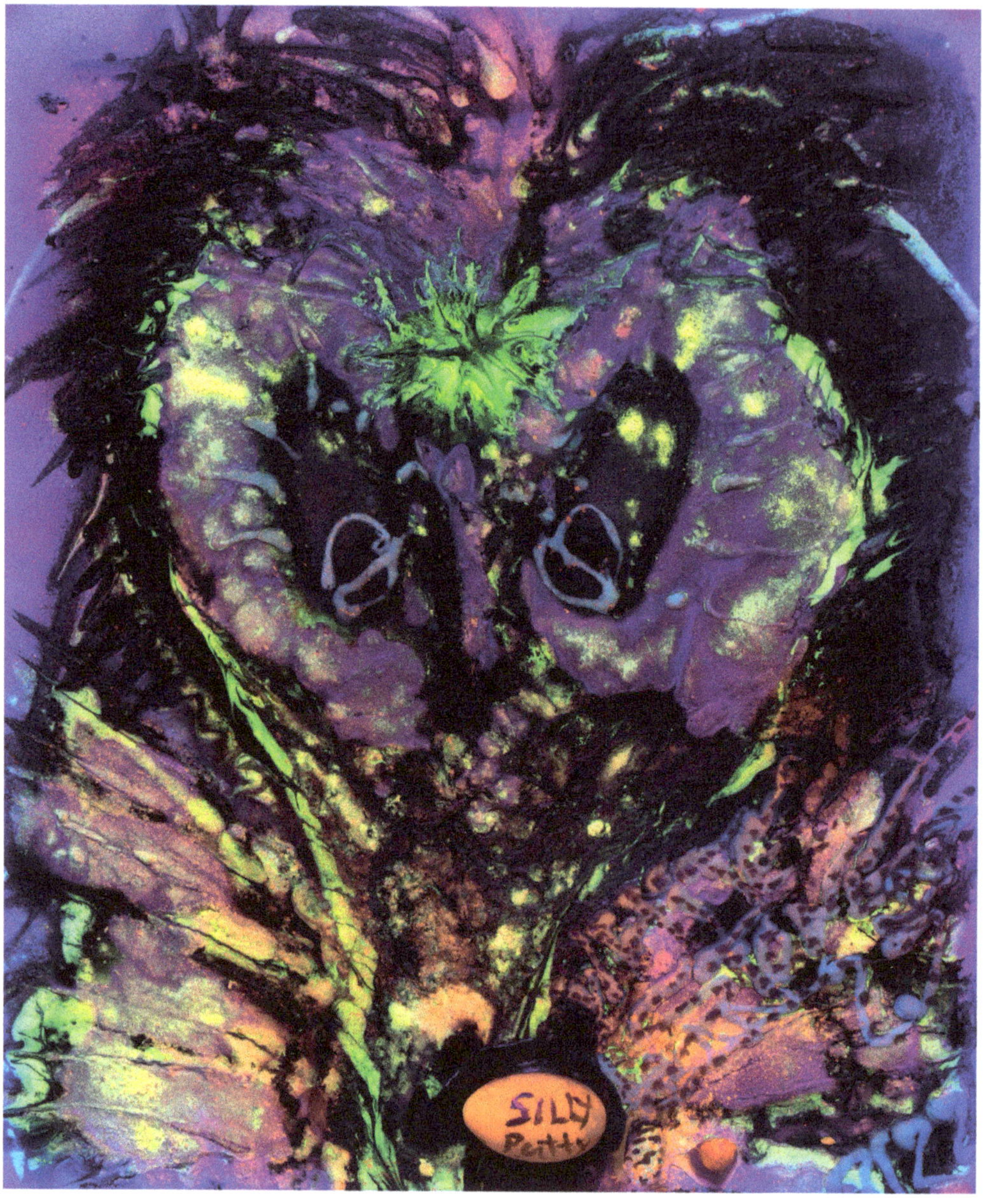

Silly Putty Glow Dog

Can you create something new from a moment of joy from your childhood?

Silly Putty Glow Dog

I created "Silly Putty Glow Dog" during one of those rare moments when I decided to let joy lead instead of intellect. I bought an egg of glow-in-the-dark Silly Putty from the local art store. It was a whimsical moment, remembering the joy of my childhood. I played with the stuff for hours when I was a kid. I needed a playful reset—and working under black light with fluorescent paint became my escape hatch from overthinking.

The violet background emerged first, glowing with that otherworldly purple that reminds me of childhood wonder—of fireflies and glow sticks and those precious summer nights when time seemed suspended in magic. I mixed the pigments intuitively, chasing that precise frequency of color that vibrates with delight rather than meaning.

That dog face wasn't planned—it materialized as I played with texture, pressing and pulling the paint like the silly putty that gave this piece its name. I remember laughing out loud when those eyes took shape, how they seemed to watch me with the same guileless curiosity my childhood dog would show when I was creating something. Those blue-white circles appeared spontaneously, reflecting the black light like little moons.

The egg of glow in the dark "Silly Putty" glued at the bottom was my surrender to whimsy—an admission that sometimes transformation comes not through profound suffering but through remembering how to play without purpose. This painting taught me that seriousness isn't the only path to depth, that joy creates its own kind of wisdom when we trust it enough to lead.

Make sure to scan the QR code because the picture here is the glow-in-the-dark version.

Compost Creation

Creativity bloomed from the compost of abandoned certainties. I once knew exactly how the world worked—or thought I did. But nature unraveled my neat explanations. The garden taught me how last year's dead leaves make this year's tomatoes juicy and sweet. What looks like a rotting mess is actually life turning itself inside out to create something new. When my sure answers fell apart, I felt lost in their decay. But from that rich, dark confusion grew ideas I never could have planned—wild, colorful thoughts reaching toward the sun. My old beliefs weren't wasted; they were transformed, like kitchen scraps into garden gold. Now, when something I believe turns out wrong, I don't panic. I add it to my heart's compost pile, knowing something unexpected and beautiful will eventually grow from what I've discarded.

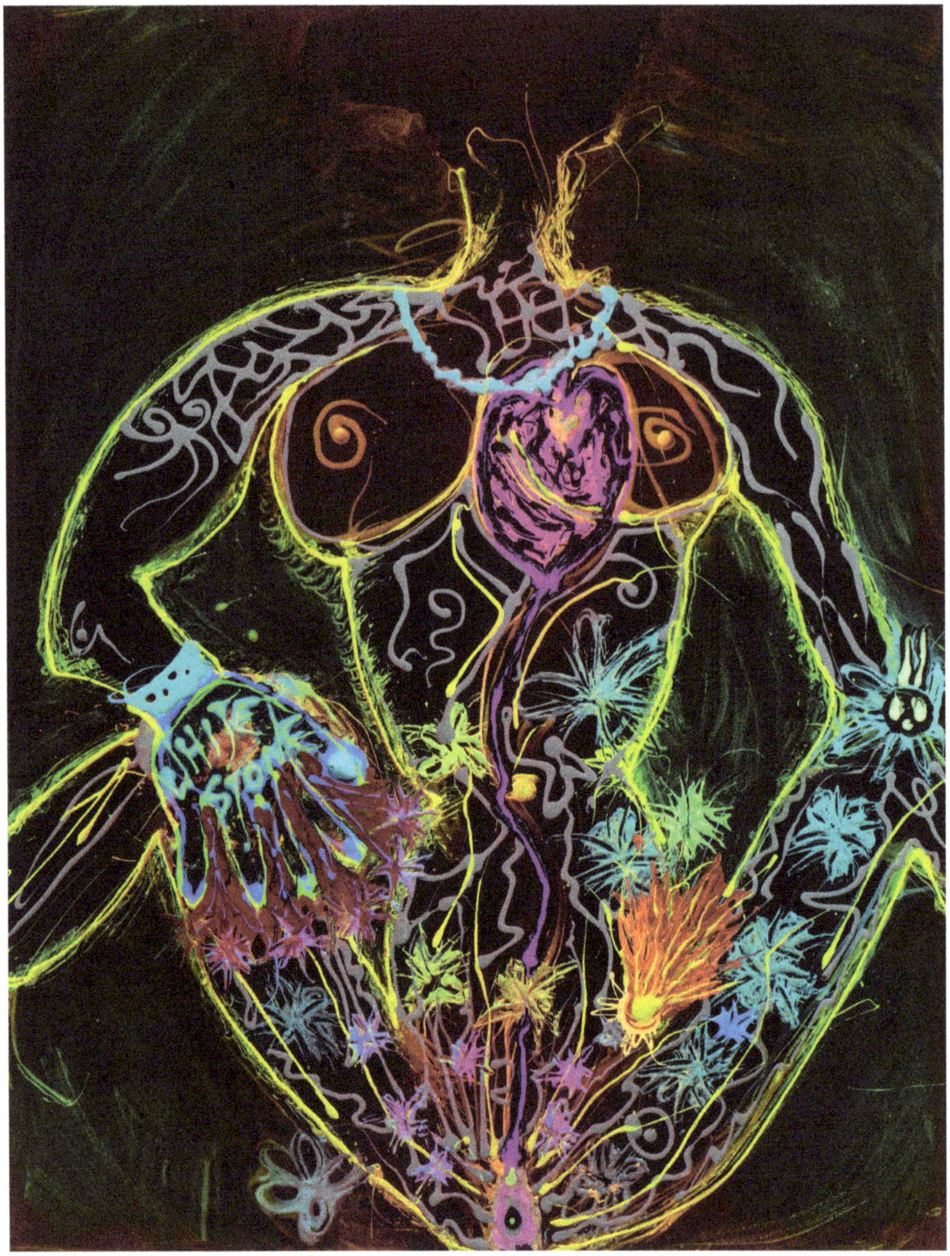

Glow Jo

Desires of the heart are fleeting until mystery has her way with you!

Glow Jo

I called this one "Glow Jo" because she emerged directly after one of the most exhilarating sexual encounters of my life. My lover's beauty flowed through me like an unstoppable current days after our tryst in my studio, compelling me to immortalize our connection. The memory of her body guided my hands as I created this first nude—a luminous testament to both sexual ecstasy and the mystical feminine energy that has both haunted and blessed my entire life. This painting stands at the intersection of physical desire and spiritual revelation, a glow-lit homage to love's transformative power and the divine gift that led me to discover my true artistic path.

My lover's glowing anatomical heart wasn't planned—it appeared organically as I drew the long crimson line connecting it to her vagina, making visible the current that ran between these centers of power and pleasure. Working under black light in a trance-like state, I channeled our shared intimacy onto canvas, creating a luminous phantom of our encounter that only we would fully recognize. The violet and magenta pulses capture both ecstasy and longing—the frustration of potential futures unrealized. My tattooed hand at the bottom serves as both signature and claim, acknowledging that this creation emerged from our mutual surrender to desire. The fluorescent blossoms blooming throughout her torso represent those moments when vulnerability transforms into unexpected joy, when darkness becomes necessary for witnessing our most luminous selves. This painting stands as testament to how erotic connection reveals hidden aspects of ourselves, allowing us to finally glow with our complete truth. Scan the QR code to see "Glow Jo" come alive in all her beauty.

Light Alchemy

The luminosity in my paintings emerged from the same source as fireflies and distant stars—the alchemy of darkness transformed. Fireflies create light through a chemical reaction inside their bodies—turning darkness into visible magic. Stars burn against the blackness of space, somehow more brilliant because of the deep dark surrounding them. My art began finding its true glow when I stopped being afraid of dark feelings or difficult experiences and instead let them become part of the chemical reaction of creation. Now, when sadness or fear visits, I don't rush to chase it away. I welcome it as potential fuel for that mysterious alchemy that transforms life's darkness into unexpected light.

Flower Bliss

Maybe if you stop asking for what you want, you'll see you're getting exactly what you need?

Flower Bliss

I began "Flower Bliss" with a profound feeling of joy and freedom. The explosion of colors was easy to drop onto the canvas, but then they erupted from some internal wellspring that had been quietly gathering strength beneath my conscious awareness. That vibrant background of yellows, oranges, and reds came first—colors that felt like celebration, like emotional sunlight breaking through clouds. It's not surprising when I turned the black light on, the painting just popped even more. Scan the QR codes to see how the flower sinks more deeply into the canvas, a reminder that even the most beautiful things in nature are birthed in the dark.

I remember feeling almost dizzy with the pleasure of pure creation, of watching form emerge from formlessness without forcing it. Those blue accents appeared spontaneously, perfect counterpoints to the warm palette, like moments of clarity punctuating euphoria.

The turquoise edges materialized as I worked outward from the center, creating natural boundaries that contained but didn't constrain the exuberant energy. Working on this square 30x30 canvas felt like the perfect container—balanced and complete, like the experience of bliss itself. Thus emerged the name "Flower Bliss."

This painting taught me that sometimes our deepest creative expressions come not from striving but from surrender, not from technique but from trust. The flower became both subject and teacher—showing me how beauty unfolds according to its own internal logic when we simply create the conditions for its emergence and then step aside in wonder.

Earth's Secrets

Earth whispered her secrets only when I ceased demanding answers. I used to stomp around the creek asking big questions out loud: "Why is water wet? Why do leaves change color? Where do rocks come from?" But the louder I asked, the less I seemed to learn. Then one day, I just sat quietly by the water. I stopped asking questions and just watched and listened. That's when amazing things happened! A blue heron landed nearby. A crawfish peeked out from under a stone. I noticed tiny bubbles making patterns in the still water. Nature began sharing all kinds of secrets, but not as answers to my questions—as gifts for my quiet attention. Earth talks very softly and sometimes with no words at all. Her deepest secrets come not when we demand them, but when we're patient enough to simply be still and notice.

Goddess of Light & Dark

There is a divine feminine present in beauty, holding mercy in her hands to insure restoration for the entire universe!

Goddess of Light & Dark

I began "Goddess of Light & Dark" when completely lost, but simultaneously curious about how I could influence the canvas. I placed a light under the canvas with wire crossing under the easel, using pencil to draw the shadow lines that came forth on the canvas above. From that point I found myself being completely led, like a divine spirit was moving through my hands, directing me to use color and strokes that would create this piece of work. I've included pictures to show my strange efforts in painting her.

The central dark silhouette emerged unexpectedly as I worked vertical strokes down the canvas. I didn't set out to create a feminine form or a dark raven lurking in the middle above her fiery arms, but there they were—a presence rising from the interplay of intention and accident. Those vivid color columns—yellow, pink, green—appeared as directed, what now seem like different aspects of feminine energy: intuition, compassion, growth. Scan the QR code and watch her come alive. This painting was one of my first, so the glow version reflects a darker side, which is why I named her the "Goddess of Light & Dark."

Working on this piece transformed my understanding of integration—showing me that wholeness doesn't require homogeneity, that light and dark don't need reconciliation so much as acknowledgment, that the divine feminine contains multitudes without contradiction. The goddess emerged not as fantasy but as recognition—a spiritual manifestation of what was already present but previously unseen.

Sky Lesson

The sky taught me to hold both emptiness and possibility in one breath. Look up at the sky—it's basically nothing, right? Just empty blue space. But that same emptiness also holds clouds, birds, airplanes, weather, and stars at night. The sky is empty and full at the same time. When I felt hollow inside after my father died, the sky helped me understand something. My sadness was like an empty blue sky, but that same space could also hold new things—memories, love, and ideas I hadn't even thought of yet. With just one breath, I could feel both the empty space and all the amazing things that might fill it someday. The sky showed me that empty places aren't just about what's missing—they're also about making room for what might come next.

West

What sets you on fire for change?

West

I tackled "West" on an expansive 36×48 canvas after returning from a transformative journey through the American southwest. Those emerald vertical lines weren't planned but erupted from my body's memory of towering desert plants—saguaros standing sentinel against endless horizon, their persistent vitality against all odds. The azure horizontal sweeps emerged as I recalled the startling presence of water in arid environments—how even the suggestion of moisture feels miraculous in parched terrain. Each blue stroke carries the emotional impact of discovering hidden creeks and unexpected oases amid seeming emptiness.

Those black accents appeared during moments of confronting shadow—both literal desert shadows that provide life-saving coolness and the psychological shadows I encountered traveling alone through unfamiliar territory. I worked them in quickly, intuitively, respecting their necessary presence in the composition of both landscape and experience. Please scan the QR code to see the landscape set on fire.

The title "West" emerged upon completion as I contemplated how certain moments in the desert are transformed by specific light—late afternoon sun igniting common rocks into temporary treasure. These chromatic memories weren't about documenting places but capturing how they altered my perception.

This painting taught me that landscape exists not just externally but internally—that "west" isn't merely directional but emotional, carrying ancestral memories of frontier, possibility, and confrontation with elemental forces.

Ash Ember

I discovered how to hold both the ash and the ember in the same open palm. After a campfire has died down, have you ever moved the gray ash covering the fire pit, but when you gently blow on one spot, an orange ember glows beneath? "Fire's not gone," you observed, "just sleeping under its blanket of ash." The gray ash of disappointment or loss might cover everything, making life seem cold and finished. But underneath, if I'm gentle enough to look, tiny embers of hope or possibility still glow, waiting for the breath of attention to brighten again. Indigenous fire-keepers know how to shelter overnight embers to start the next day's fire without matches. I'm learning to carry both— the reality of life's cold ashes and the treasure of hidden sparks—in the same open palm, neither denying the loss nor abandoning the possibility of warmth returning.

Mighty Glow Bird

When was the last time you wasted time doing something you've never done before?

Mighty Glow Bird

The mighty bird that emerged at the bottom of this painting came from a significant amount of spilled paint on that spot. The radiant orange-yellow background wasn't planned either but erupted from some deep well of excitement within me—maybe like the precise color of dawn breaking after a long darkness. I applied it with sweeping gestures, letting my imagination run wild with absolutely no expectation of any particular result. Scan the QR code to watch the "Mighty Glow Bird" take flight in a new light.

Those crimson pathways emerged organically as I wanted something deep inside me to be connected to the process of creation. Satisfaction emerged as I began to see patterns forming with the use of ongoing texturing. The blotch of paint, as mentioned, materialized as the mighty bird. I didn't set out to create a creature, but there it was—wings spread in defiance or celebration, its form both rising from and embedded within the textured field. The directional movement felt like both flight and rootedness, my ongoing theme of "Flying Grounded" appeared once again.

Those starburst formations scattered throughout the composition emerged as I experimented with pressing objects into wet paint. This painting taught me about the relationship between vastness and detail—how expanding my physical gesture to match the canvas size revealed miniature worlds within the broader strokes. The mighty bird isn't separate from its environment but constituted by it, just as my own identity isn't isolated but formed through relationship with everything that surrounds and sustains me. I also learned that mistakes could be transformed into something useful.

Absence Cradle

I learned to cradle absence as the womb of what waits to be born. When the big oak tree in our yard got struck by lightning and had to be cut down, all that was left was a giant empty space. I'd sit in that space and feel sad, missing how the tree gave shade and homes to squirrels. But then spring came, and sunlight could finally reach that spot on the ground. Wildflowers bloomed there like never before—purple ones and yellow ones making a bright patch of color. Birds came to eat seeds from the flowers. The empty space wasn't just empty—it was making room for new life that couldn't have grown in the tree's shadow. I started to see the hole in our yard like a nest or a cradle, holding possibility. Now when I lose something, I try to rock that empty space gently, wondering what new thing might be getting ready to grow there.

PART FOUR

Breathing Through the Storm

*"Breathing is the greatest pleasure in life. Art is
the second greatest."* —Marty Rubin

The Invitation of Wild Air

In the cathedral of ancient redwoods, breath transforms. Something fundamental shifts when lungs fill with air filtered through needles and moss, carrying molecules that have danced with bark and stone. The forest exhales what we inhale; we exhale what the forest receives—an exchange as old as our species, yet forgotten in the sealed chambers of our constructed lives.

The first time I truly breathed in nature—consciously, deliberately—I felt my ribcage expand beyond its familiar boundaries. The membrane between inner and outer worlds thinned to transparency. My breath, previously shallow and constricted, deepened into the earth beneath my feet, drawing up something primal and necessary that had been waiting to be remembered.

We have forgotten how to breathe. In our climate-controlled rooms, before our glowing screens, within the grip of perpetual urgency, our breath has become a hostage—shallow, anxious, interrupted. We take in just enough air to survive but not enough to fully inhabit our lives. This constricted breath reflects our constricted awareness, our narrowed perception, our diminished capacity for presence.

Nature dismantles these restrictions with quiet insistence. Stand before the vast indifference of an ocean, and the lungs demand fuller expansion. Walk a winding mountain path, and breath synchronizes with footfalls, creating a rhythm older than language. Sit beside a stream's unceasing movement, and your breathing slows to match its patient persistence. These are not poetic coincidences but physiological recalibrations—the body remembering its original dialogue with the living world.

The Language of Emotional Weather

As breath deepens in wild spaces, something remarkable surfaces—emotions rise like weather systems across an inner landscape. Feelings long submerged beneath the ice of productivity and propriety begin to thaw, to move, to speak. Nature's emotional honesty—its storms and sunbreaks, its deaths and renewals—grants us permission for our own emotional truth.

I have wept beside alpine lakes for no defined reason, felt joy pulse through me at the sight of unfurling ferns, encountered rage while watching a thunderstorm reshape the sky. These emotions weren't about the landscape but were revealed by it—as if the expansiveness outside created corresponding space within.

This emotional emergence carries a curious paradox: as feelings intensify, they become less personal. The sorrow that rises while watching autumn leaves release from branches connects to a grief both universal and ancient. The wonder that blooms while witnessing stars emerge against darkness connects to a wordless reverence that has lived in human hearts across millennia. Our emotions, given room to breathe, reveal themselves not as private burdens but as flowing tributaries of a shared emotional watershed.

This recognition transforms our relationship with feeling itself. No longer something to manage or overcome, emotions become messengers carrying vital information, guides illuminating values and boundaries, teachers offering wisdom from our depths. What emerges is not emotional turbulence but emotional fluency—the capacity to read and speak the complex language of our inner weather without being destroyed by its storms.

The Bridge of Breath

Between the wild world and our wild inner landscape stands the bridge of conscious breath. The simple act of following breath—its entrance and exit, its rise and fall, its texture and temperature—creates a threshold between thinking and being, between naming and experiencing.

In meditation, we discover breath as both anchor and vehicle. It roots us to the present moment while simultaneously conveying us deeper into unexplored territories of consciousness. With each inhalation, something of the world enters us; with each exhalation, something of ourselves returns to the world. This continuous exchange dissolves the illusion of separation, revealing a permeable boundary between self and other, inner and outer, known and unknown.

As attention rides the rhythm of breath, something remarkable unfolds—the thinking mind, with its ceaseless categorizing and commentating, begins to quiet—not through force or suppression but through gentle redirection, like a parent guiding an overtired child toward sleep. In this quieting, spaces open between thoughts, gaps widen between words. And in these openings, imagination stirs.

Not imagination as we commonly conceive it—the deliberate construction of fantasy—but imagination as a deeper perceptual capacity. This imagination perceives patterns and possibilities invisible to conventional awareness, senses connections between seemingly unrelated elements, receives rather than imposes meaning. This receptive imagination flourishes in the fertile silence between thoughts, in the rich darkness beneath the conscious mind.

Seeds in Darkness

Our creative essence dwells in shadow. Beneath the cultivated gardens of our conscious identity, below the domesticated landscape of our familiar thoughts, exists a wilderness—untamed, fertile, alive with movement. We fear this inner darkness, avoiding it through noise and distraction, forgetting that all seeds require darkness to germinate.

When breath carries awareness into these depths, we discover that what appeared threatening from a distance becomes fascinating up close. The shadows we feared contain not monsters but mysteries, not dangers but dormant gifts. Like eyes adjusting to nightfall, our inner perception gradually reveals detail and dimension in what initially seemed uniform darkness.

This inner wilderness operates by different laws than our conditioned thinking. Where the conscious mind proceeds linearly, this deeper awareness moves in spirals and unexpected leaps. Where rational thought constructs from known elements, this subterranean knowledge grows like mycelium, an interconnected system sensing nutrients and possibilities beyond our limited perception.

Nature demonstrates this principle constantly. The forest floor, appearing dormant and unchanging, thrums with invisible recreation. Fallen trees decompose into soil; seeds await specific combinations of moisture and temperature; fungi transmit messages and nutrients between seemingly separate organisms. Creation requires periods of apparent inactivity, intervals of darkness and dissolution, before new forms emerge.

Our imagination follows similar patterns. Ideas need dormancy before germination. Insights require incubation. Creative visions develop in darkness before they're ready for light. By honoring these rhythms—by breathing into our depths without demanding immediate results—we align with the natural cycles of creation and recreation that govern all living systems.

The Art of Contemplative Presence

Nature offers masterclasses in presence. The heron standing motionless at the water's edge, the wolf attentively scanning its territory, the turtle basking in sunlight—these beings demonstrate a quality of attention increasingly rare in human experience. They inhabit time differently, without the fragmentation of multitasking or the distortion of anxiety about past and future.

When we bring this quality of presence into our human lives, everything transforms. Tasks previously rushed through become opportunities for full engagement. Conversations deepen as we listen with our entire being rather than preparing our next statement. Creative work shifts from striving for outcomes to surrendering to process, allowing the work to reveal what it wishes to become.

This contemplative presence illuminates aspects of our lives previously hidden in the blur of speed and habit. We begin noticing which activities drain our energy and which replenish it. We recognize relationships that constrict our breath and those that invite expansion. We discern the difference between genuine satisfaction and temporary distraction, between choices aligned with deeper values and those driven by conditioned patterns.

These recognitions arise not through analytical thinking but through embodied awareness. The body knows what brings fulfillment—it responds with relaxation, with deeper breathing, with subtle sensations of rightness and alignment. The body equally knows what diminishes well-being—it contracts, restricts breath, generates signals of discomfort or discord. Learning to read these somatic communications provides guidance more reliable than conceptual understanding alone.

The Breath of Self-Care

At its essence, self-care begins with breath—not the commodified version of self-care marketed as products to purchase or services to consume, but the fundamental act of attending to your own living presence. The simple question, "How am I breathing right now?" opens a door to authentic self-care more powerful than any wellness routine.

Constricted breath reflects constricted life energy. When breathing becomes shallow and tight, it signals that something needs attention—a boundary requiring protection, a need going unmet, a truth seeking expression. By noticing these patterns without judgment, we develop the capacity to respond skillfully to our own needs rather than abandoning ourselves in the face of external demands.

Conscious breathing initiates a cascade of physiological benefits: activating the parasympathetic nervous system, reducing stress hormones, improving immune function, enhancing cognitive clarity. But beyond these measurable effects lies a deeper restoration—the return to embodied presence after periods of dissociation, the reclamation of internal authority after deferring to external expectations, the remembering of wholeness after fragmentation.

Invitations to Reconnection

The journey toward breathing through storms—both external and internal—begins with simple practices that gradually expand awareness beyond conditioned limitations. Consider these invitations as trailheads rather than destinations, initial steps on a path that unfolds according to your unique internal landscape:

Dawn Breath Ritual: Before engaging with devices or responsibilities, step outside barefoot for three minutes. Feel the earth beneath your feet as you take ten conscious breaths, expanding your awareness with each inhalation to include more of the living world around you. Notice one natural detail you've never perceived before.

Weather Walking: Choose one day each week to walk in "bad" weather—rain, wind, snow, intense heat. Experience how different atmospheric conditions change your breathing patterns and emotional states. Rather than resisting these changes, explore them with curiosity. What textures of feeling emerge in each weather system?

Breath Cartography: Create a breath map of your home and workplace by noticing how you breathe in different locations. Mark spaces where breath naturally deepens and areas where it becomes restricted. Consider how to bring elements from the former into the latter, or how to spend more time in places that invite respiratory openness.

Creation Through Exhalation: Begin a creative session with five minutes of attention to the exhalation phase of breathing. With each outbreath, imagine releasing not just air but expectations, judgments, and preconceptions about what you're about to create. Allow the emptying process to create space for something unexpected to emerge.

Emotion Breathing: When strong feelings arise, experiment with breathing directly into the bodily location where the emotion manifests—the clenched jaw of anger, the hollow chest of grief, the fluttering stomach of anxiety. Instead of naming or analyzing the feeling, simply surround it with breath awareness, creating space for its movement and expression.

Nature Mirroring: Find a natural element that attracts you—a particular tree, stone, water feature, or vista. Visit it regularly through changing seasons and weather conditions. Notice how it responds to different circumstances without resistance. Practice breathing in rhythm with this element, allowing its qualities to inform your presence.

Threshold Breathing: Establish a breathing ritual for crossing thresholds—the doorway to your home, the entrance to your workplace, the boundary between wilderness and civilization. Use breath to consciously mark these transitions, releasing the energy of the space you're leaving and preparing to fully inhabit the space you're entering.

The Continuing Storm

We live in stormy times—environmentally, politically, socially, personally. The temptation to armour ourselves against these storms through numbness or distraction grows increasingly powerful. Yet protecting ourselves from life's intensity simultaneously shields us from its beauty and meaning, from the creative potential born in turbulence.

Breathing through storms requires tremendous courage—the willingness to remain open when everything within and around us urges closure, to maintain presence when dissociation offers immediate relief. This courage develops gradually through practice, through thousands of moments of choosing to breathe with rather than withdraw from experience.

The breath-centered life is not one of perpetual calm or absence of difficulty. Rather, it's a life increasingly capable of remaining in conscious relationship with whatever arises, of continuing to breathe fully even as winds intensify and foundations shake. This capacity allows us to navigate deeper currents beneath surface turbulence, to access creativity and compassion when they're most needed yet seemingly least available.

In the end, breathing through the storm isn't about controlling internal or external weather but about discovering yourself as both the storm and the witnessing awareness—vast enough to contain all weathers, rooted enough to withstand all winds, fluid enough to flow through all transitions. With each conscious breath, this knowing deepens: you are both the changing shapes of clouds and the unchanging sky through which they move, both the surging waves and the depths untouched by surface commotion.

And in this recognition lives a profound peace that doesn't deny turmoil but includes it within a larger, wilder wholeness—a peace available with every breath that remembers itself as part of something immeasurable and alive.

Haunted Forest

What scares you should get your attention.

Haunted Forest

My teacher Aviva Gold, of Painting from the Source, always encouraged us to paint, paint, paint. She often said, "It's okay to start over or paint over a previous work." I know of an artist who buys used paintings and paints over the existing art for inspiration and affordability. This may seem taboo to other artists, but the truth is: nothing lasts forever. After my vision quest, I was moved to use a canvas, asking the group to add their own strokes of paint to the painting. When all swiped a color across the surface, I lit it on fire. Everything starts with nothing and can easily return to nothing.

From the spirit of this idea and just before Halloween, I painted the "Haunted Forest" (inspired by the photo below) over a previous piece of work. I welcomed the ghostly white spaces arising from the acrylic tile cement I used as texturing. The tree trunks emerged naturally as I layered and pulled the paint and paste downward, creating the sensation of peering into depths where vision falters, where known becomes unknown. These intervals of emptiness became as important as the solid forms—the negative spaces where imagination projects its own apparitions. I sprayed a coat of glow spray paint on top as I moved downward which created the hints of acid green within the darkness. This connection demonstrated how what frightens us often glimmers with strange life and curiosity. This painting taught me that sometimes we must render our fears visible to recognize their beauty, that what haunts us carries wisdom alongside warning. The forest isn't merely threatening but truthful—a landscape where opposites coexist without resolution, where boundaries between self and other, known and mystery, protection and peril dissolve into something more authentic than certainty.

Wilderness Studio

The studio became another wilderness where I continued my descent into the luminous unknown. My little art room with its paint-splashed floor turned out to be just as wild as any forest I had walked through. The blank canvas stood like an unexplored mountain, each tube of paint a stream running with possible colors. Some days, I felt lost among my own brushes and jars—confused, worried, not knowing which path to take. Other days, I discovered surprising joy, like finding a hidden waterfall after hours of difficult hiking. The mess of spilled paint became beautiful like fallen autumn leaves. My mistakes turned into happy accidents, like when you slip in mud but land somewhere with a better view. In this indoor wilderness, I learned the same lessons the outdoor one had taught me—to trust the journey even when I couldn't see the destination, to find beauty in unexpected places, and to let myself be changed by the landscape I was creating. The studio walls disappeared when I worked deeply, and I felt as free as standing on a mountaintop with wind in my hair.

Strawberry Moon

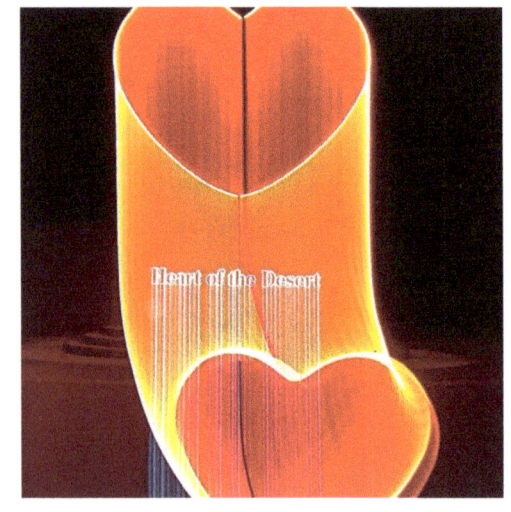

Have you ever waited for a full moon cycle to make a decision?

Strawberry Moon

I painted "Strawberry Moon" during that rare June evening when the full moon rose blushing with unexpected tenderness, mirroring some awakening vulnerability within me. The silvery pearl-white background came first—laid down in whispered layers that captured that liminal quality of twilight when the world hovers between defined and dissolving. Make sure to scan the QR code to see the moon take flight in the dark.

That magnificent coral-rose orb felt like it was birthed in my surrender to its beauty. The textured surface appeared as I built translucent glazes, each one containing tiny golden flecks, like memories embedded within emotions, experience crystallized into light.

The aquamarine waters below formed naturally as counterpoint, that necessary balance between celestial and terrestrial, between aspiration and grounding. I worked these cerulean ripples during predawn hours when my rational mind had finally quieted enough to let my hands remember how water holds light—not by grasping but by receiving, by allowing transformation through reflection.

This painting taught me that creation mirrors natural cycles—that sometimes we must wait through darkness for the exact moment of emergence, that what appears simple from a distance reveals intricate complexity upon closer viewing, that what we create isn't separate from but continuous with what we experience. The strawberry moon doesn't just illuminate the landscape—it becomes part of it through reflection, just as our interior light transforms what we perceive.

Glowing Edges

The glowing edges of my creations echoed the liminal spaces where I had met my truest self. Painting the summer strawberry, I noticed the most interesting part wasn't the sun itself but the reflection on the ocean, like glowing lines where light and shadow met. These in-between spaces vibrated with energy and mystery. My life's most powerful moments happened in similar threshold places—neither one thing nor another but the electric edge between. Twilight, shorelines, doorways—these boundary spaces have been considered magical in cultures worldwide. The Celtic tradition calls them "thin places" where the veil between worlds grows transparent. My art began capturing these glowing edges—not just visually but emotionally: the trembling space between joy and sadness, the threshold between knowing and mystery, the luminous boundary where "me" meets "not-me." Now I intentionally seek these liminal spaces in both life and art—the dawn moments, the season changes, the heart-opening transitions—knowing these thresholds where worlds touch are where the most truthful light gets in, illuminating edges that glow with their own special magic.

Glow Stone Lake

When was the last time you took a walk in the forest at night and alone?

Glow Stone Lake

"Glow Stone Lake" felt like dreaming on canvas. The emerald canopy emerged first, summoned from my memories of standing beneath trees where dappled light transforms ordinary moments into encounters with the sacred. I worked with fluorescent pigments that would later transform under black light, creating a painting that exists in multiple realities simultaneously. Make sure to scan the QR code to see the glow lake emerge from the dark.

Those vertical trunks appeared as I meditated on boundaries—how forests both protect and isolate, how they create sanctuary while marking the threshold between known and mystery. The luminous lake basin formed what felt like a safe gathering place for reflection and swimming at night. I added the blue glow stones popping from the canvas around the lake to bring more focus to the water's edge.

This painting taught me that creativity requires both cultivation and surrender—the deliberate tending of technical skill alongside the willingness to step aside and allow something unexpected to emerge through us rather than from us. The glow stone lake exists not just as an image but as an invitation—a doorway into seeing everyday landscapes transfigured by attentive presence.

Sacred Ground

Between surrender and becoming lies the sacred ground where creativity whispers its true name. When a caterpillar enters its chrysalis, it doesn't just grow wings. Scientists discovered it actually dissolves into soup before reforming as a butterfly! That in-between state—no longer caterpillar, not yet butterfly—is where the magic happens. I experienced this after trying so hard to be good at basketball and finally surrendering that dream. In the quiet let-go space that followed, with no pressure to be anything specific, I found myself drawn to painting in ways I'd never expected. Native Americans honor "liminal spaces"—thresholds like shorelines, where ocean meets land, or dawn, when night becomes day. These in-between zones buzz with creative energy. Now I recognize that feeling of hovering between what I've released and what I'm becoming as holy ground. I take off my shoes of expectation and wade barefoot into that sacred space, listening for creativity's quiet voice telling me who I might become next.

Beauty of Chaos

Can you see the beauty in chaos through emotional surrender?

Beauty of Chaos

I began "Beauty of Chaos" after returning from a wander in the Pacific Northwest. I brought to the studio the chaos of the weather that seemed to just rip through the Oregon Coast. That coral-salmon background emerged first, reminding me of a dawn breaking after emotional darkness, a hue that carried both warning and promise.

Those explosive teal and charcoal gestures erupted from some primal wellspring where words fail but movement speaks truth. The stormy shoreline colliding with the mammoth green, wet forest felt like destruction and creation existing not as opposites but as accomplices in transformation. Each chaotic stroke embodied my wild memories of standing on the edge of the cliffs, wondering how time and weather had shaped the mysterious landscape. Scan the QR Code to see how chaos can glow.

The golden sun broke through the clouds—a perfect circular stillness amid turbulence, revealing how chaos often organizes itself around quiet centers. I applied this ochre orb, anticipating how it might bring a needed hope to the scene.

Those russet-amber swirls that snake through the composition materialized as the image of a mythic creature arising from rivers, formed from oceans. When finished, I could imagine how new channels through resistant terrain often find an unexpected route toward something mystical. This painting taught me to recognize beauty not despite chaos but within it—how disorder contains emergent patterns, invisible to controlling consciousness but apparent to surrendered attention. It brought the faith I needed to embrace uncertainty as a creative principle rather than a problem. Now I claim the beauty of chaos as a theme for all my work.

Lost Sacred

The wilderness taught me that being lost is sacred orientation. I panicked when I couldn't find the path back—heart racing, feet scrambling. But as shadows lengthened and I accepted I was really, truly lost, something shifted. I began noticing details I'd missed: moss growing thicker on the north side of trees, the evening star appearing, ants returning home in straight lines. Being lost made me see better, listen closer. Indigenous people sometimes seek vision by getting lost on purpose—they call it "finding your true direction." When maps and plans fall away, we discover how to navigate by deeper truths: intuition, observation, connection. Now when I feel lost, I treat it as a doorway to better orientation. Instead of frantically searching for the old familiar path, I look around with fresh eyes, noticing new guides and signs that were there all along, waiting for me to become properly lost enough to see them.

SWOOSH!

How flexible and resourceful are you at changing direction and going with the flow?

SWOOSH!

I discovered "SWOOSH!" not through careful planning but through playful archaeology in my unconventional studio—the transformed basement of a century-old Prescott apartment building. This unexpected creative sanctuary emerged from what was once merely a maintenance room and storage area, its utilitarian past still echoing through the space.

The painting's voice first whispered to me as I rummaged through abandoned maintenance tools—mops, chains, and wire—that previous caretakers had left behind. These forgotten implements became my co-conspirators, offering unexpected pathways into expression that traditional brushes could never provide. The distinctive rhythmic pattern materialized when my hands found a rounded piece of wood among the basement's treasures. Something about its weathered surface called to me, suggesting movement beyond what my conscious mind had imagined. I loaded it with color and rolled it across the canvas in sweeping arcs, watching as it translated physical momentum into visual energy.

The textured organic field bubbling along the bottom emerged later as counterpoint, grounding the sweeping motion above in something more primal and earthy. This tension between movement and foundation, between soaring and rooting, transformed a simple experiment in motion into a complete visual ecosystem.

What began as playful curiosity with found objects became a lesson in creative possibility—how the humblest tools can catalyze the most profound expressions when approached with openness rather than predetermined expectation. The basement's hidden treasures taught me that sometimes we must look not for what we think we need, but for what unexpectedly awaits our discovery. Scan the QR codes to feel the painting's motion.

Hollow Reed

I became a hollow reed through which the wind of mystery played its forgotten melodies. Walking through tall grasses one fall day, I found a broken reed and blew across its open end. The sound surprised me—clear and haunting. Later, I sat very still by the marsh and noticed how wind made music through those hollow plants. They didn't create the song; they simply allowed themselves to be instruments. This is what I learned to do with myself. When I emptied my mind of noise and opinions, when I cleared my heart of what I thought should happen, something greater could flow through me—like wind through that reed. The most beautiful things I've created came not from trying harder but from getting out of the way. The universe has songs to sing that need human instruments. We just need to become hollow enough, still enough, to let ancient melodies pass through us untampered.

From Me to You

How does your mind keep you isolated and addicted to loneliness?

From Me to You

I began "From Me to You" during a season of profound disconnection, when isolation had crystallized into something that felt permanent rather than temporary. That vibrant coral-red background emerged first, not from planning but necessity, pulsing with the exact frequency of longing, a color that somehow captured both wound and healing simultaneously.

This painting expresses how I often feel about myself and others, between isolation and communion. This visual dialogue between pronouns revealed the painting's deepest truth: that separation is an illusion, that loneliness exists only within a greater communion, waiting to be recognized.

Those twelve blue flower-like formations appeared organically around the perimeter, calling to mind ancient sacred geometries of protection and guidance. Each one emerged with its own character, its own voice, yet together they formed a perfect celestial council surrounding the central figure—guardians witnessing our human journey, neither judging nor rescuing but simply present through all our transformations.

This work taught me that creative expression isn't merely personal catharsis but universal invitation—a bridge extending from isolation toward connection, a reminder that every "me" exists in relationship to countless "yous" even when we cannot sense their presence in our more contracted moments. Scan the QR code to see how we are all connected through light.

Ancient Gestures

My hands remembered ancient gestures my mind had forgotten—how to summon light from shadow. Painting without thinking one afternoon, my fingers moved in circular motions I hadn't planned. The resulting spiral pattern felt strangely familiar—like a movement my hands had always known. Looking later at ancient pottery designs from cultures around the world, I found that same spiral everywhere—in Greek vases, Native American ceramics, African carvings. My hands had remembered what my mind never learned. Scientists say our bodies carry "muscle memory" beyond our conscious awareness. Artists throughout time have used similar gestures to bring forth light and form from nothingness. These movements live in our shared human inheritance—like how we instinctively know to rock a crying baby or reach toward warmth. When I trust my hands' ancient wisdom instead of only following my thinking brain, my art connects to something older and deeper than my individual life. Now when creating, I sometimes close my eyes, letting my fingers remember these primordial gestures that have summoned beauty from darkness since the first human hands shaped clay or pressed pigment against cave walls.

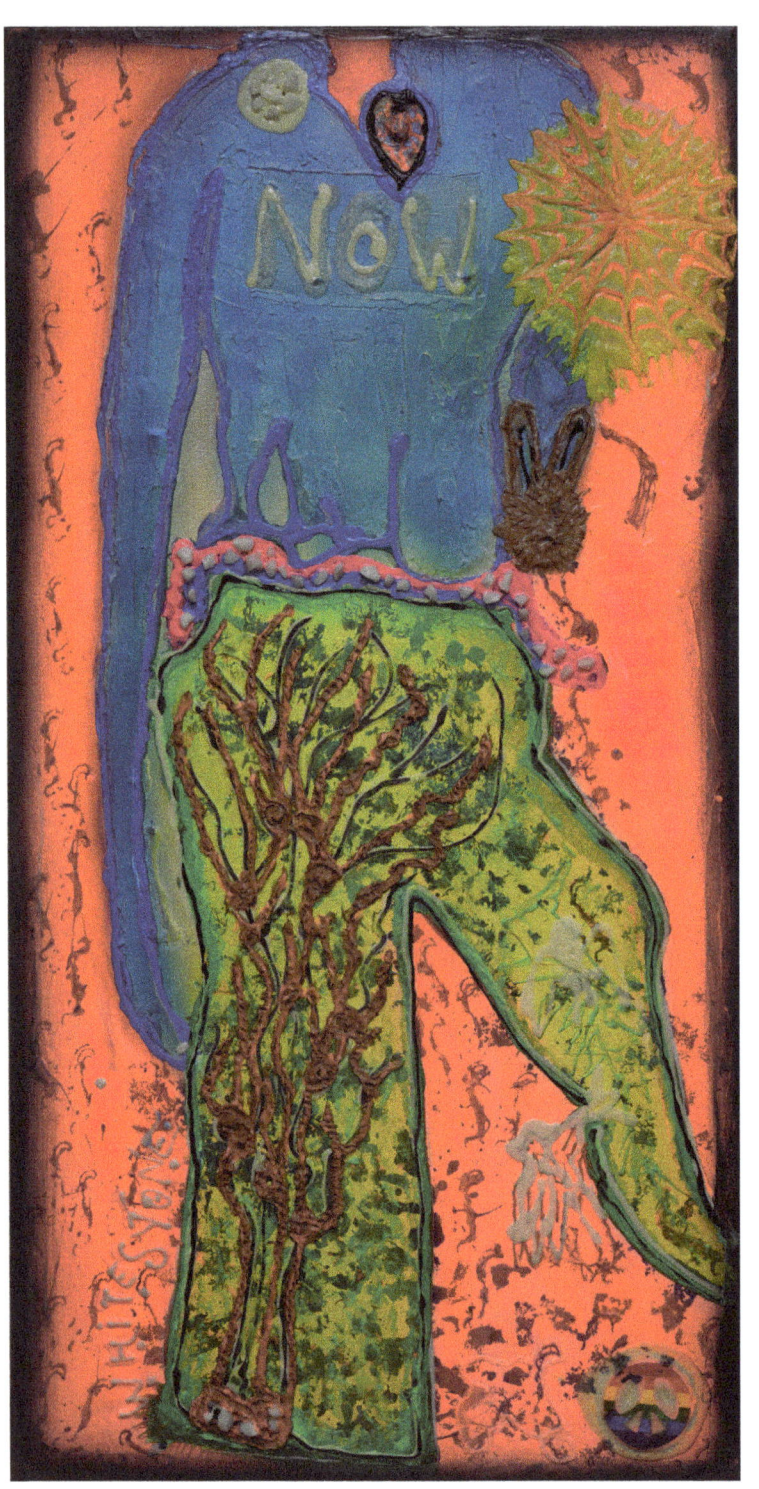

Peace Now

If you desire peace, you must devour yourself first.

Peace Now

I painted "Peace Now" as my first conscious self-portrait—not of outer appearance but inner landscape. The vibrant coral background emerged not from planning but as volcanic emergence, the exact hue of transformation that precedes acceptance. This chromatic intensity carried both the fire I'd once fled and the warmth I finally embraced after encountering Bill Plotkin's "Wind Mind" teachings.

The blue figure arose not from intellect but from something elemental—a manifestation of that mythic poetic identity, Whitestone, that had emerged earlier on my journey. "NOW" appeared across the chest during that liminal dawn between thinking and being, crystallizing my deepest understanding that peace exists not as a distant horizon but as an immediate presence. The tree extending from the leg represents my wanderings through forest and desert—how the animate world is both mirror and teacher, showing me that rootedness and reaching are complementary movements of the same life force. These natural rhythms taught me that authentic peace requires both grounding in earth wisdom and openness to sky possibility. Once again one of my painting themes appeared, fly grounded.

I revised this painting in 2025 from its original by adding more glow and color. Through Aviva Gold's guidance that "we are all artists," I discovered that the blank canvas offers the same pristine potential as each moment of existence—an invitation to transform emotional intensity into visible presence, to alchemize judgment into expression. What began as a self-portrait became self-revelation: that everything I'd judged or fled contained sacred fire necessary for creation, that peace emerges not by transcending humanity but by fully inhabiting it—canvas by canvas, breath by breath, moment by precious moment.

Echo Canyon

I became both the silence and the echo in the canyon of transformation. Shouting into the big canyon, I heard my voice bounce back—but it sounded different, like someone else answering. I tried again, this time listening more carefully to what came back. The weird thing was, I started to feel like I was both the person shouting and the echo returning. The space between them—that quiet moment before my voice came back—felt important too. Life changes us like that canyon changed my voice. When hard times bounce against us, what returns isn't exactly what we sent out. The empty space where transformation happens became as important to me as either voice. Now when difficult things happen, I try to be patient in that echo-waiting place, curious about what might come back, knowing I am both the caller and the responder in this deep canyon of growth.

PART FIVE

The Dance of Emotions: Understanding the Essential Role of Both Positive and Negative Feelings

"In art, the hand can never execute anything higher than the heart can imagine." —Ralph Waldo Emerson

The Sweet and Bitter Banquet

We approach our emotional lives like children let loose in a candy store, grabbing handfuls of sweetness while avoiding anything with a hint of bitterness. We fill our pockets with joy's colorful confections: contentment's smooth chocolate, enthusiasm's fizzy pop rocks, love's rich caramel, hope's cotton candy dissolving into possibility. Who wouldn't prefer these delights to the sharp licorice of grief, the bitter dark chocolate of anger, the sour twist of disappointment?

Yet this selective feasting creates an unexpected hunger. The more we avoid emotional complexity, the more our capacity for genuine fulfillment shrinks. Like a landscape painted only in pastels, our inner world becomes flat, lacking the contrast and depth that gives existence its full dimension.

What if our sweetest experiences can only reach their full potency when balanced by their shadowed counterparts? What if joy's summit can only rise as high as sorrow's depth has carved space for it to grow?

The Fertile Soil of Difficult Emotions

Our cultural narrative portrays negative emotions as weeds to be eliminated from our emotional garden. We're taught to uproot fear, prune back anger, mow down sadness, and spray disappointment with positive-thinking herbicide. Yet these emotions aren't invaders—they're essential elements of our inner ecosystem, as necessary as fungi in forest soil or microbes in a healthy gut.

Consider how our primary challenging emotions serve not as obstacles but as catalysts for our most transformative experiences:

Fear: The Edge Where Growth Begins

Fear appears at the boundary between what we know and what we're becoming. That flutter in your chest when trying something new, the contraction in your throat before speaking your truth, the hesitation before stepping into vulnerability—these are not warnings to retreat but invitations to expand.

Fear whispers, "Here is your growing edge."

Without fear, courage remains theoretical. The mountain climber standing at the base of an imposing peak feels fear's electric current run through her body—and in choosing to climb anyway, she discovers capacities previously dormant. The artist facing the blank canvas experiences the stomach-dropping fear of inadequacy—and in continuing to create despite this feeling, finds expression that transcends limitation.

Fear doesn't merely enable courage—it actively calls it into being. Each time we breathe through fear rather than back away from it, we expand our capacity to hold intensity without becoming overwhelmed by it.

Sadness: The River that Carves Capacity for Joy

Sadness arrives as heaviness, as hollowing, as the tender ache that reveals what matters most. When tears come for what's lost or what never came to be, they carve channels through our emotional topography—riverbeds that, once created, remain available for joy's flowing abundance.

Consider how the parent who has wept over a child's suffering experiences a depth of appreciation unavailable to those who've never felt such vulnerability. I have a friend who's teenager was diagnosed with epilepsy. She's wept many times over her daughter's difficult visits to the doctor, to the loss of being able to drive and other restrictions that have been put on her at such an early age; yet she becomes overjoyed when they finish a hike without passing out.

Sadness whispers, "This matters deeply."

Our tears are not signs of weakness but evidence of our capacity for connection. Each time we allow ourselves to fully feel loss or longing rather than numbing or deflecting it, we expand our ability to experience life's corresponding sweetness with equal depth.

Anger: The Fire that Forges Boundaries and Peace

Anger arrives as heat, as electrical charge, as the clarifying burn that illuminates where boundaries have been crossed or values violated. The flush rising to your cheeks when witnessing injustice, the tightening of your jaw when disrespected, the surge of energy when something important is threatened—these are not defects of character but vital signals from your inner compass.

Anger whispers, "This line matters."

Without anger's intelligence, peace becomes mere passivity. The activist who channels righteous anger into structural change, the partner who expresses clean anger rather than silent resentment, the artist whose creative fire transforms rage into revelation—these demonstrate anger's constructive potential when honored rather than suppressed.

Anger doesn't oppose peace but creates the conditions for genuine harmony based on truth rather than compliance. Each time we allow anger's energy to move through us without becoming destructive, we develop the capacity for boundaries that foster authentic connection.

Disappointment: The Compost that Nourishes Authentic Satisfaction

Disappointment arrives as deflation, as the collapse of expectation, as the gap between what we imagined and what materialized. The sinking feeling when efforts don't yield desired results, the hollowness when experiences fall short of anticipated joy, the questioning that follows paths not taken—these are not failures of manifestation but essential elements in developing discernment.

Disappointment whispers, "Realign with what truly matters."

Without processing disappointment, satisfaction remains shallow and fleeting. The entrepreneur whose failed ventures informed successful innovation, the seeker whose spiritual disillusionment led to authentic practice, the creator whose rejected work sparked more genuine expression—these illustrate how disappointment composted becomes wisdom.

Disappointment doesn't prevent satisfaction but refines our understanding of what genuinely fulfills us. Each time we metabolize disappointment rather than avoid or deny it, we develop more accurate inner guidance toward meaningful achievement.

The Integration Journey: Creating Wholeness

Our emotional well-being depends not on eliminating difficult feelings but on developing a mature relationship with the full spectrum of human experience. This integration happens not through intellectual understanding alone but through embodied practice—repeatedly turning toward rather than away from emotional complexity.

Here's how this transformative journey unfolds:

1. Emotional Literacy: Reading the Inner Landscape

Like learning to read terrain before hiking wilderness trails, emotional literacy involves recognizing patterns and features in our inner topography. This begins with simply naming what arises—not as judgment ("I'm feeling bad") but as specific identification ("This is disappointment, located in my chest, with a heavy quality").

This naming creates crucial space between experiencing an emotion and becoming identified with it. Just as saying, "I notice anger arising," differs fundamentally from, "I am angry," emotional literacy establishes the perspective that allows conscious relationship rather than automatic reaction.

Developing this literacy means learning particular emotional dialects—how anxiety manifests in your body, how grief moves through your system, how joy registers in your awareness. These patterns are as unique as fingerprints, requiring patient observation rather than conformity to external descriptions.

The emotionally literate person navigates inner storms with the same respect and attentiveness a sailor brings to changing weather—not controlling the elements but reading their signals to respond appropriately. This literacy transforms emotional experiences from threats to be managed into information to be integrated.

2. Emotional Resilience: Weathering Inner Storms

Resilience develops not by avoiding emotional intensity but through regular, supported exposure that builds capacity gradually—like muscles strengthened through appropriate resistance. Each time we breathe through fear instead of backing away, stay present with grief instead of distracting ourselves, or feel anger's energy without acting impulsively, we expand our window of tolerance.

This widening capacity creates freedom. The resilient person isn't someone who never feels difficult emotions but someone who can experience their full intensity without becoming overwhelmed or destructive. This resilience then allows positive emotions to be felt with equal depth and authenticity rather than serving as mere coverings for unprocessed pain.

Like a tree that develops stronger roots when exposed to wind, emotional resilience grows through engagement with challenge. The flexibility to bend without breaking, to feel fully without fragmenting, to recover balance after disruption—these capacities emerge not despite difficulty but because of our willingness to engage with it consciously.

3. Emotional Depth: Creating Dimensional Experience

A photograph needs both highlights and shadows to capture dimensional reality. Similarly, our emotional experience requires full-spectrum awareness to reflect life's true richness. This depth emerges when we recognize that seemingly opposite emotions often coexist and even complement each other—the bittersweet nature of watching children grow, the tender grief within profound gratitude, the vulnerability inseparable from deep love.

Emotional depth reveals the artificial nature of our categories. Joy and sorrow aren't opposing forces but different expressions of the same capacity for feeling. Anger and compassion aren't contradictory but complementary aspects of caring deeply. Fear and excitement share nearly identical physiological signatures, differing primarily in the stories we attach to sensation.

The emotionally deep person experiences life not as flattened into "positive" or "negative" but as richly textured with multiple dimensions simultaneously present. This complexity creates a fullness of experience unavailable to those who fragment their emotional landscape into acceptable and unacceptable territories.

Nature's Teachings: Embracing Emotional Wholeness

The natural world offers profound guidance for navigating emotional complexity. Unlike human systems that often pathologize or hierarchize emotional states, nature demonstrates continuous integration of seemingly opposite forces—destruction and creation, darkness and light, death and birth—as essential aspects of a single living process.

Here are three nature-based practices for embracing your complete emotional spectrum:

The Seasonal Emotions Practice

Choose a natural location you can visit regularly through changing seasons. Commit to experiencing this place in all conditions—spring bloom, summer heat, autumn decay, winter stillness. During each visit, bring awareness to your full emotional weather without preference or judgment.

In spring's emergence, notice both hope's expansion and the vulnerability this openness creates. In summer's fullness, experience both abundance's joy and the subtle anxiety of impermanence within peak experiences. In autumn's release, feel both the melancholy of letting go and the relief of surrendering what's complete. In winter's dormancy, attend to both the discomfort of apparent emptiness and the restful potential of fallow periods.

This practice reveals how emotional states naturally cycle rather than progress linearly toward permanent positivity. It demonstrates that each season brings gifts unavailable in others, teaching us to value our internal winters and summers equally as essential aspects of wholeness.

The Elements Integration Ritual

Find a location where multiple natural elements are present—ideally water, earth, fire (or sun), air, and wood. Identify a challenging emotion present in your experience—perhaps fear, anger, grief, or disappointment. Instead of trying to transform this emotion, explore how each element might help you relate to it differently:

Water: How might this emotion flow if given permission to move rather than remain static? Place hands in water (stream, bowl, or rain) while breathing with this question.

Earth: How might this emotion be held with the steady containment earth provides? Place palms or bare feet on soil, sensing its solid support beneath intensity.

Fire/Sun: How might this emotion's energy be recognized as a vital force rather than a problem? Feel sunlight or safely contained fire's warmth, noticing its transformative quality.

Air: How might this emotion create space for new perspective when given breath? Feel wind or breath moving across skin, experiencing its capacity to create both intensity and relief.

Wood: How might this emotion participate in your growth like weather-shaped trees? Touch living wood, noticing how trees incorporate rather than resist the forces acting upon them.

This practice helps us recognize emotions not as isolated internal events but as energies in the larger field of natural forces. It reveals how different aspects of the natural world offer metaphors and models relating to emotional states with curiosity rather than resistance.

The Atmospheric Emotions Meditation

Find a vantage point with an expansive sky view—perhaps a hilltop, open field, or water's edge. Settle into a comfortable position where you can observe changing conditions above. Bring awareness to your current emotional state without attempting to modify it.

As you observe the sky, notice how atmospheric conditions continuously change—clouds forming and dissolving, light shifting quality, colors transforming, weather systems moving through. Notice how these changes occur without resistance, how the sky neither clings to clear conditions nor rejects stormy ones.

Recognize your consciousness as this sky-like awareness—the spacious presence within which all emotional weather moves. Practice maintaining connection with this expansive quality even as you fully experience whatever emotions arise, neither suppressing nor becoming identified with any particular state.

This meditation reveals the paradoxical truth that we are both the changing weather of our emotions and the unchanging awareness that witnesses this weather. It cultivates the capacity to fully feel without becoming defined by any emotional state, recognizing that like atmospheric conditions, all feelings naturally arise, transform, and dissolve when given space to move through their complete cycle.

The Wholeness Beyond Categorization

The pursuit of perpetual positivity fragments our experience, creating artificial boundaries between aspects of our humanity that naturally exist as integrated wholeness. When we release this fragmentation, we discover something remarkable—our capacity for joy, love, and contentment actually expands proportionally to our willingness to embrace their shadowed counterparts.

This is the paradox at emotional integration's heart: what we resist persists, while what we embrace transforms. The emotions we judge as negative don't disappear when rejected but go underground, emerging later in distorted forms. When welcomed with conscious awareness, these same emotions reveal their wisdom and naturally complete their movement through our system.

The emotionally whole person doesn't experience fewer difficult feelings but relates to all emotions with equal presence, neither clinging to pleasant states nor rejecting challenging ones. This equanimity creates freedom not *from* feeling but *for* feeling everything, allowing emotional energy to fulfill its natural function as messenger and motivator rather than becoming stuck in patterns of avoidance or identification.

Like the natural world, our emotional landscape thrives not through simplification but through diversity, not through control but through relationship, not through permanent stability but through continuous transformation within. By embracing this wholeness—this complete spectrum of human experience—we discover not the limited happiness of perpetual positivity but the unlimited aliveness of authentic presence with whatever arises, moment by moment, breath by breath, season by changing season.

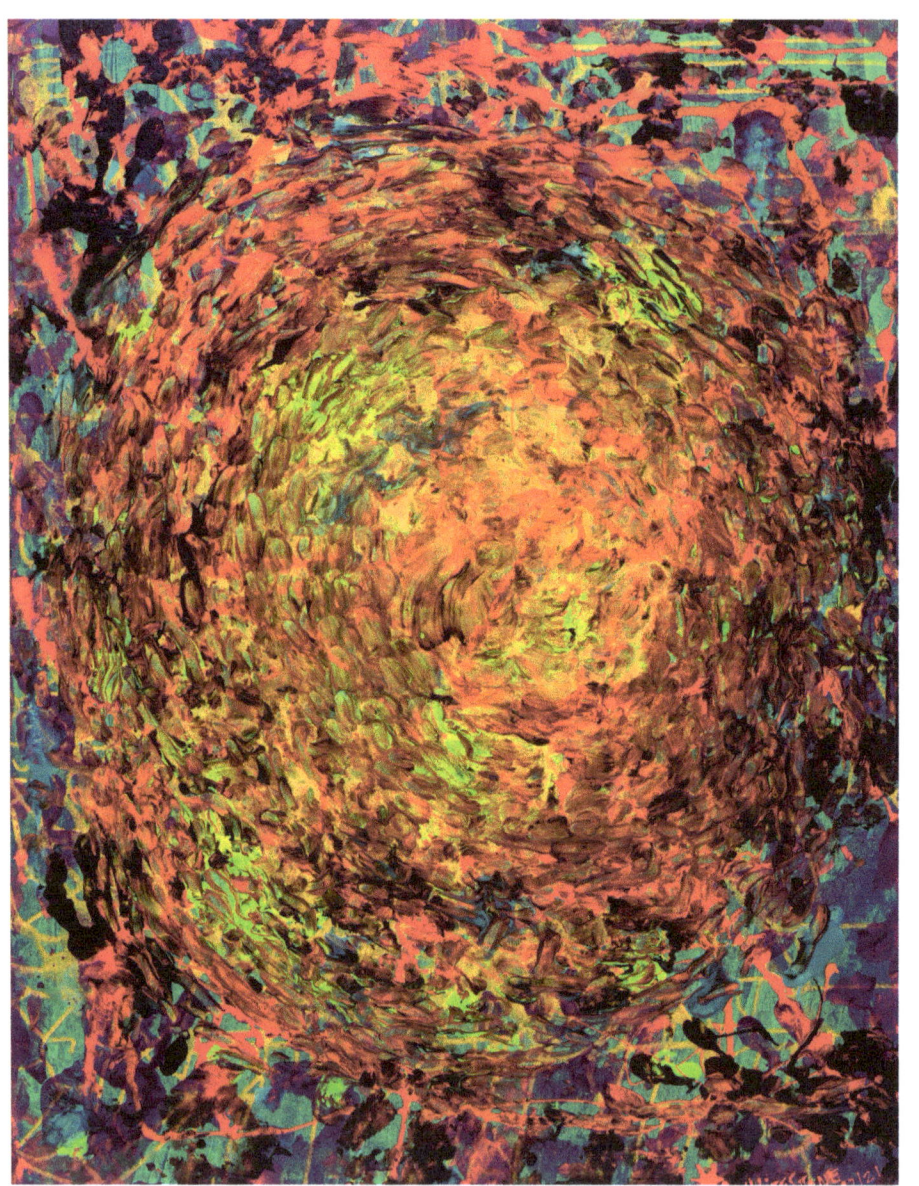

Sassy Nest

Have you created a sacred space for nesting in your home?

Sassy Nest

"Sassy Nest" was my exploration of a sassy mess. I've always been drawn to the circle as a spiritual container where everything has a beginning, a middle, and an end. The kaleidoscopic edges emerged first—an explosion of turquoise, magenta, and electric green that refused containment or apology. What started with splashes of paint on canvas turned into an invitation to use my hands and let the spirit move in circular patterns. This is a declaration of my creative wildness breaking free.

The central nest-like vortex emerged as a total surprise, as I remembered my time in the wilderness compiling images and embodied patterns of gathering, building, and protecting. I surrendered to something beyond conscious intention, watching as my hands created a spiral sanctuary amidst chromatic chaos.

The textural complexity developed as I layered and scraped, built up and carved away—mirroring how nests are constructed from countless individual elements, each seemingly insignificant alone, yet crucial to the structural integrity of the whole. These staccato marks and fractured surfaces created their own visual rhythm, a pulsing energy field surrounding the central calm. Scan the QR code to see the original colors and how the black light version of this pictured emerged.

What began as abstract exploration transformed into a profound meditation on home—not as a physical location but as an internal state, a center we carry within that remains intact despite external turbulence. The sassy, vibrant perimeter serves not just as decoration but as a fierce boundary, a joyful declaration that sometimes protection of our essential nature requires both softness and spectacular display.

Spiral Trust

I learned to trust the spiral path that seems to lead nowhere. Hiking the canyon trail, I grew frustrated with all its twists and turns. "Why not go straight up?" I complained. But then I noticed something: spirals are everywhere in nature—from snail shells to unfurling ferns, from whirlpools to galaxies swirling in space. Nothing in nature moves in straight lines for long. The spiral path that seemed so wasteful actually made the climb gentler, showed me views I'd have missed on a direct route, and followed the land's natural flow. Now when my life feels like it's going in circles—passing the same problems again and again—I remember the spiral's wisdom. Each loop brings me to a similar place but at a different level, like climbing a mountain one switchback at a time. The path isn't lost; it's just more beautiful than straight.

Grow To Glow

What you judge as broken may be the only way the light shines through.

Grow To Glow

"Grow To Glow" is about broken patterns emerging as something new and whole. It was a free-form exploration of how everything somehow fits together. It's a celebration of color and one of my first real glow paintings. Those fluorescent swirls and cosmic bursts were not planned but erupted from some primal place beyond thought. The electric color palette emerged through experimentation with blacklight-reactive pigments, allowing the painting to exist simultaneously in multiple realities—one version visible in ordinary light, another revealed when ultraviolet frequencies transform the surface into something otherworldly. This duality became a perfect metaphor for growth itself—how we contain both visible manifestation and hidden potential, how transformation often begins in dimensions others cannot yet perceive. Each luminous loop carries its own rhythm, some tight and concentrated, others expansive and reaching, together creating visual ecology where diverse patterns coexist without hierarchy. Scan the QR code to see the original version of the painting.

The starburst formations scattered throughout materialized as I contemplated moments of sudden illumination—those instances when growth accelerates beyond gradual evolution into quantum leaps of understanding. The explosive nodes represent not just external achievement but internal revelation, the exact sensation when perspective shifts and everything previously seen transforms into something new.

This canvas taught me that true growth doesn't distinguish between process and outcome—the growing and the glowing are simultaneous rather than sequential, each moment containing both becoming and being. The painting's vibrant chaos mirrors how authentic development rarely follows predictable patterns but instead emerges through joyful surrender to our most radiant possibilities.

Loss Geometry

In the geometry of loss, I discovered expansion's hidden mathematics. When my business of 30 years came to an end, my world felt smaller, shrunken by what needed to dissolve away. But standing in the empty space, I felt a new freedom. I started wandering at night. The stars seemed brighter, the moon more inviting. Nature's strange math lesson revealed itself: sometimes losing one thing multiplies another. The exact shape of what's missing creates a perfectly sized hole for something new to enter. Like sand dollars and sunflowers that follow sacred patterns, loss has its own beautiful geometry. Now, when something disappears from my life, I look for what expands in its absence. Empty spaces aren' just about what's gone—they're also perfect outlines for what might be arriving, following equation-patterns too big for us to solve.

Birds of Paradise

Do you have a flow state? What are you willing to sacrifice to find or be in it?

Birds of Paradise

I created "Birds of Paradise" as a delayed revelation from my 2014 vision quest in the crimson canyons of Capitol Reef. For four days, I'd lived at the edge of known existence—just water, tent, journal, and the vast Utah wilderness surrounding me. What began as solitude transformed into communion as hundreds of birds enveloped me in their kingdom, their songs rewiring my consciousness until the boundary between human observer and avian collective dissolved entirely. The phosphorescent bursts and spectral blossoms capture how my imagination made everything sing and fly. The emerald backdrop mirrors the paradoxical lushness I discovered within arid canyon walls, where scarcity revealed hidden abundance.

The luminous green circles containing flame-like centers appeared spontaneously as I worked, representing portals between worlds—gateways between ordinary and non-ordinary reality that opened during those desert nights when the veil between realms grew permeable under star-scattered skies. This canvas stands as testament to mystery's patience—how seed experiences may wait decades before blossoming into visible expression, how the most profound initiations reveal their meanings gradually through our willingness to listen beyond human language.

Scan the QR code to see the original and glow version of the work.

Vessel Pouring

I became both the vessel and the pouring—the canvas and the radiance seeking form. Watching water flow from pitcher to cup, I realized something about creativity—I wasn't just the pitcher (the artist) pouring ideas onto canvas (the cup). I was also the water itself, flowing from one shape to another. And strangest of all, I was the cup, too, receiving and holding what came through. Many spiritual traditions use vessel imagery to describe how humans both contain and channel something larger than ourselves. The Sufi poet Rumi wrote about being "the flute that the breath of God plays through." When I stopped seeing myself as separate from my art—as just the maker standing apart from what I made—something shifted. Colors flowed more truthfully, forms emerged more honestly. I was simultaneously the container, the contained, and the act of pouring from one to another. Now when creating, I remember this fluid trinity—how I am the artist, the art itself, and the mysterious process flowing between them—all at once the clay, the potter's hands, and the wheel's momentum carrying both.

Glow Guardian

Have you ever wanted the freedom to fly like a bird in the sky?

Glow Guardian

I painted "Glow Guardian" after a revelatory period in my decade-long journey of descent—part of an unexpected covenant with the avian world that found me. This rose-copper sentinel emerged not through planning but recognition, materializing from textured layers as if it had been waiting patiently within the canvas for my hands to uncover it.

For years, birds had been inserting themselves into my life as constant companions and teachers. The owls that faithfully appeared before night wanderings and the silent witness perched outside my window as I wrote poetry, the hawks that drew my eyes skyward during canyon hikes. I found myself regularly climbing to high vantage points, seeking to understand terrain through their perspective, curious about how they navigated both sustenance and shelter. The emerald starburst centers within this guardian figure became luminous nodes representing wisdom gathered through observation rather than analysis—teachings that arrived through presence rather than pursuit.

What fascinates me is how I've never deliberately set out to paint birds. They simply manifest within the mysterious patterns that emerge on empty canvases, appearing through some intelligence beyond my conscious direction. Each one arrives as both surprise and recognition—a visual confirmation of the paradoxical wisdom they've been teaching me all along: "Fly Grounded." Scan the QR code to see how comforting this wild one becomes in the dark.

This painting stands as testament that sometimes we must descend deeply into our interior landscapes before we understand what it means to soar. The guardian's watchful presence reminds me that protection often comes from unexpected sources when we remain receptive to mystery's unfolding invitations.

Trembling Trust

I learned to trust the trembling line that wanders without destination, like my feet in the wilderness. Trying to draw perfectly straight lines for my building sketch, my hand shook, making wobbly marks I hated. But looking at tree branches against the sky, I noticed nature doesn't use rulers—every line in the living world quivers with energy. The most interesting paths aren't straight but winding, responsive to what they encounter. When I stopped forcing my lines to be perfect and instead let them tremble honestly, my drawings came alive with the same energy I felt walking uncertain trails through the forest.

Rio (1 of 3)

Have you merged your mind with the living forest within you?

Rio (1 of 3)

I painted "Rio" as a sensory translation after my transformative journey to the Ciranda Retreat Center near Rio de Janeiro. Those cascading vertical textures emerged first, feeling a sensation of standing within the rainforest, where the ominous trees become both veil and revelation, obscuring ordinary sight while unveiling deeper perception.

Under Carioca's masterful musical guidance, my awareness was fundamentally altered. The rhythms unlocked doorways beyond conventional hearing, allowing me to perceive the actual vibrational signatures of the living forest—frequencies that exist just beyond ordinary human perception. The crimson streaks throughout the composition reflect those moments when sound became visible, when sensory boundaries dissolved completely. Scan the QR code to see this painting come to life with changing light.

The bird-like forms appeared spontaneously as I worked, materializing not through deliberate representation but through embodied memory—how certain movements during forest ceremonies momentarily dissolved the distinction between human and avian consciousness. These figures capture that extraordinary sensation of simultaneously inhabiting ground and sky, limitation and freedom.

This painting stands as a living testament to how landscapes transform us when we approach them with receptivity rather than merely as observers—how Rio's unique confluence of music, forest, and ceremony continues to reverberate through my creative expression long after my physical return.

Of Stones and Storms

The wilderness taught me to speak in the tongue of stones and storms. When I was alone in wild places, I learned to understand the rocks and rain. I listened with my whole body to the old, old stories that mountains tell. Storms showed me that it's okay to be loud and real—thunder doesn't apologize for being noisy, and lightning doesn't hide its bright flash. Before, I used to talk like people expected me to, being polite and careful with my words. But outside in nature, my voice remembered how to be true and simple, like when I was little. I discovered that real talking doesn't come from fancy words but from being honest about what's inside me. The wilderness helped me learn this forgotten way of speaking. It showed me that before I could really talk to others, I needed to get comfortable with quiet moments. I had to let go of all my made-up stories and find the real, simple truth inside—the kind that doesn't need big words to be understood.

De (2 of 3 Rio Series)

There is a time for weeping every minute of the day.

De (2 of 3 Rio Series)

I painted "De" under black light as the second in my Brazilian trilogy, channeling experiences that transcended ordinary consciousness at Ciranda near Rio. Those electric green swirls seemed to be tracing the vibrational signatures of jungle entities I'd encountered during the ceremony led by Carioca and other master musicians.

The fluorescent patterns capture how perception transforms in the rainforest. Those emerald spirals map the energetic pathways I perceived when sound became visible, when conventional senses merged into synesthetic experience. Scan the QR code to see the jungle come alive with changing light.

The shadow figures embody knowledge systems that exist beyond intellectual grasp but can be momentarily accessed through altered states. The pulsing crimson and magenta regions reflect those moments when temporal perception collapsed—when I briefly experienced the rainforest not as a current ecosystem but as ancient intelligence that has witnessed millennia of planetary evolution. The chromatic zones mark instances where linear time briefly surrendered to something more circular and comprehensive.

What fascinates me is how working under ultraviolet light mirrors the ceremonial experiences themselves—how certain truths remain invisible until viewed through alternative frequencies of perception, how reality shifts depending on which wavelengths we're capable of receiving. The painting glows with information that remains hidden until proper conditions reveal it—just as the jungle's deepest wisdom emerges only when approached with appropriate reverence and receptivity.

Earth Holding

Earth held me when I could no longer hold myself together. When tears came hot and fast after the big disappointment, I dropped into the forest and lay in the mystery of its darkness. The ground caught me without question or judgment. It absorbed my wet grief like summer rain. I pressed my mind's eye deeper into my inner landscape and felt the planet spin beneath me, holding me in its massive gravity hug—the same embrace that holds oceans in their beds and clouds in their skies. Earth has been catching falling things since time began: meteors and leaves, raindrops and exhausted animals. That night, it caught me too. I didn't have to be strong or make sense. I just had to surrender to being held by something infinitely patient. When we can't keep ourselves together, the ground remembers how to hold our pieces until we're ready to gather them again.

Janeiro (3 of 3 Rio Series)

Shifting consciousness is a unique human gift. Just imagine how you find it.

Janeiro (3 of 3 Rio Series)

I completed "Janeiro" as the culminating piece in my Brazilian trilogy—a luminous homage to the avian beings that transformed my understanding of consciousness during my time at Ciranda. This fluorescent bird form materialized not through planning but through embodied memory. Those electric aquamarine swirls surrounding the central figure emerged as I contemplated how birds exist within multiple dimensions simultaneously—navigating physical space while inhabiting vibrational realms beyond human perception. These spiral patterns map the invisible air currents and energy fields I briefly perceived during ceremonial states at Ciranda, when ordinary boundaries of awareness temporarily dissolved. Scan the QR code to see the original and glow versions.

The bird's heart center glows with that distinctive neon green—the exact frequency of life force I witnessed pulsing through the rainforest at dawn, when the boundary between night and day created momentary portals between worlds. This luminous core reveals how my heart serves as the primary organ of perception when I move beyond intellectual understanding.

This final canvas in the trilogy completes a visual testament to how authentic interaction with the wilderness doesn't merely add to our experiential inventory but fundamentally rewires perception itself—altering not just what we see but how we see.

Open Hands

My hands, once clenched around certainties, now open like wings of a bird catching the morning breeze for flight. When I was younger, I gripped my opinions so tightly my knuckles turned white. I needed to be right about everything. But watching birds take flight—these wild creatures open their wings and plunge into flight—I saw a different way of being. Many wisdom traditions use open palms as a symbol of receptivity and trust. I practiced opening my hands physically when I felt mentally stubborn, and something shifted inside me too. Certainties I'd clutched began loosening their hold. New ideas found space to land in my open mind. Questions felt welcome instead of threatening. Now, when I feel myself gripping too tightly to how things "should be," I look at my hands and consciously relax them, remembering those early rising birds with wind beneath their wings, drinking sunshine and morning dew, ready to receive unexpected gifts.

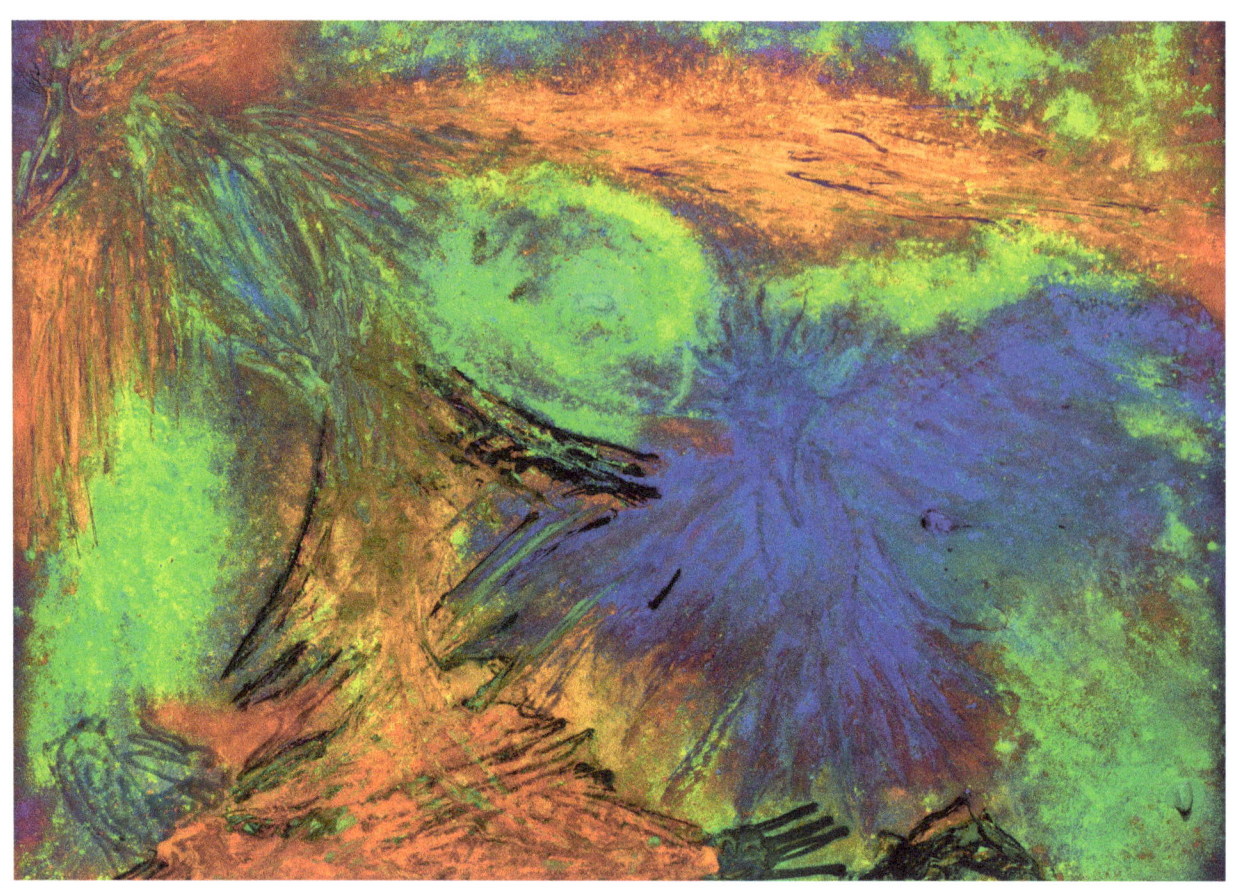

Kauai Night Flight

Is it time to take a vacation from stale thoughts that lead to stale emotions?

Kauai Night Flight

I created "Kauai Night Flight" after profound communion with one of Earth's most extraordinary landscapes. The luminous surface emerged first—layers of fluorescent pigments that capture the island's unique electromagnetic presence, that peculiar glow that seems to emanate from Kauai itself rather than merely reflect external light.

Those fiery coral-orange regions materialized as I meditated on the island's volcanic origins—how ancient lava flows continue to shape not just physical terrain but energetic currents that pulse through everything that grows there. My hands instinctively traced the molten pathways, remembering how the island feels simultaneously primordial and alive, both ancient history and ongoing creation.

That cobalt-blue burst spreading across the right side emerged as I recalled night flights of native birds. The dark marks are necessary counterpoints, representing how shadow and mystery remain essential elements of Kauai's beauty, how certain aspects remain deliberately concealed from casual observation. Scan the QR code to see the black light version emerge. My glow techniques had not yet taken hold.

My work here is a testament to how Kauai functions not merely as a geographic location but as an initiatory landscape—a place to surrender to its mysteries. What began as external documentation gradually revealed itself as internal mapping—charting not just the island's contours but the altered consciousness that emerges through my deep relationship with wild places.

Uprooted and Reconnected

When I first came to this place, I felt like a plant pulled up from the ground. My roots were cut off and I was scared. But something strange happened as I sat quietly on the earth day after day. I felt the dirt beneath me telling me stories—old stories from long, long ago. As tree roots reach deep into the ground for water, my heart reached down for those ancient stories. They made me feel strong again, but in a new way. It wasn't like before when I thought I knew everything. This was different. Now my roots go deeper than ever, drinking up wisdom that's been in the soil since before my grandparents' grandparents were born. The earth remembers everything, and now I can feel those memories flowing up through me like water through a thirsty plant. I'm still me, but I'm also connected to something much bigger and older than myself.

PART SIX

The Art of Emotion: How Embracing Feelings Fuels Creativity and an Extraordinary Life

> "Art washes away from the soul the dust of everyday life." —Pablo Picasso

Across the boundless canvas of human existence, emotions flow like rivers through the landscape of our being—sometimes gentle streams of contentment, sometimes raging rapids of passion, sometimes the deep, still pools of contemplation. Each feeling, whether illuminated by joy's golden light or shrouded in sorrow's blue shadows, offers itself not merely as experience but as raw material for creation. When we learn to touch these emotions with gentle curiosity rather than fearful avoidance, they transform from mere internal weather into the essential elements of artistic alchemy.

Try Painting Your Emotional Landscape

Imagine your emotions as terrain waiting to be mapped through color and form. Begin with a blank canvas—this emptiness mirrors the open field of awareness where feelings first arise. Select colors that resonate with your current emotional state, not through intellectual analysis but through bodily knowing. Let your hand reach for the blue that feels like today's melancholy, the crimson that pulses with your unexpressed anger, the gold that glimmers with unexpected joy found in morning light.

Don't plan or sketch. Allow your brush to become an extension of your feeling body. Perhaps begin with broad strokes that express the underlying emotional current—sweeping arcs of color that establish the atmosphere of your inner weather. Notice how certain emotions invite particular movements: anxiety might create tight, repetitive patterns; contentment might flow in gentle curves; exhilaration might explode in dynamic splashes.

As layers build upon the canvas, watch how emotions reveal their complexity through interaction. See how grief's deep indigo finds unexpected resonance with gratitude's emerald green where they meet at the edges. Observe how the terrain of feeling isn't composed of isolated states but of continuous dialogue between seemingly opposite experiences.

This isn't about creating "good art." It's about allowing emotions to become visible, to move from internal experience into external expression where they can be witnessed, honored, and understood in new ways. The canvas becomes a mirror reflecting not just what you feel, but how those feelings create the unique geography of your inner world.

The Alchemy of Emotion into Art

Every artistic medium offers a different vessel for emotional transformation. Like ancient alchemists working with fundamental elements, artists transmute the formless energy of feeling into structures that can be shared, experienced, and preserved beyond the moment of their genesis.

Painting doesn't merely capture emotions through color and form—it creates a visual field where invisible internal states materialize into tangible presence. The canvas holds what words cannot express: the simultaneous layers of contradictory feelings, the textural quality of emotional experience, the way joy can contain threads of melancholy or how anger often masks deeper vulnerability. Through brushstrokes, splatter patterns, color fields, or meticulous detail, painting offers emotions a body to inhabit outside our own.

Music weaves the unspoken through time rather than space, creating emotional narratives that unfold through melody, harmony, rhythm, and silence. A single sustained note might hold the essence of longing; a rhythmic pattern might embody the persistent return of certain thoughts; a harmonic progression might mirror the resolution of inner conflict. Music's ephemeral nature paradoxically allows it to capture the fluid, temporal quality of emotions as they arise, intensify, transform, and dissolve.

Writing structures emotions through language, creating containers that both honor their complexity and make them accessible to understanding. The writer's craft transforms chaotic internal experience into coherent expression, not by simplifying feelings but by creating frameworks that reveal their intricate architectures. Through metaphor, narrative arc, character development, or direct reflection, writing gives emotions a voice that speaks beyond the limitations of ordinary communication.

Poetry distills emotional experience to its essential nature, using language not just as representation but as incantation. The poet moves beyond description into evocation, creating linguistic structures that don't merely name feelings but conjure them into being within the reader's body. Through compression, rhythm, metaphorical thinking, and precise imagery, poetry captures what lives in the spaces between defined emotional states—the subtle transitions, the paradoxical combinations, the ineffable qualities that elude categorization.

Dance channels emotion directly through the body, honoring the fundamental truth that feelings are never merely mental events but always embodied experiences. The dancer doesn't interpret emotion but becomes its living expression, allowing the body's wisdom to articulate what the thinking mind cannot grasp. Through movement, spatial relationship, tension, release, and kinesthetic resonance, dance returns emotions to their original language—the wordless knowing of the sensing body.

Theater creates containers where multiple emotional perspectives can coexist simultaneously, allowing us to explore the complex interplay between different aspects of experience. Through character, dialogue, conflict, and resolution, theater externalizes our inner multiplicity, giving form to the various emotional "voices" that comprise our psychological landscape. This externalization allows us to witness ourselves from new vantage points, recognizing patterns and possibilities previously hidden from awareness.

Simple Exercises to Explore Emotions Through Painting

Try Painting Emotional Weather

Begin by imagining your current emotional state as weather. Is it a thunderstorm of frustration? A clear blue sky of contentment? A foggy morning of uncertainty? Gather painting materials that allow fluidity—watercolors work particularly well for this exercise—and create an abstract representation of this internal weather system.

Begin with the background atmosphere, using broad washes of color to establish the dominant emotional tone. Then add the specific elements of your weather: perhaps sharp lightning strikes of anger, gentle rain of sadness, or bright sunbursts of unexpected joy. Don't aim for literal representation but for capturing the feeling-sense of your emotional climate.

As you paint, notice how the weather constantly changes. Allow your emotional state to evolve on the canvas just as it shifts within you, moment by moment. Perhaps what began as a representation of anxiety transforms into curiosity as you engage with the process. Let the painting document this journey rather than fixing a single emotional state.

Try Painting Your Body's Emotional Map

For this exercise, begin with an outline of a human form—either drawn freehand or traced from a simple body template. Close your eyes and scan your physical body, noticing where different emotions currently reside. Perhaps anxiety creates tightness in your chest, joy bubbles in your belly, sadness weighs in your shoulders, or peaceful presence grounds through your feet.

Using colors intuitively associated with these feelings, paint these emotional locations within the body outline. Don't overthink your color choices—trust your instinctive associations. Areas of intense emotion might have more saturated colors or thicker application of paint; subtle feelings might appear as transparent washes or delicate marks.

This visual body map reveals how emotions exist not as abstract concepts but as lived, physical experiences. The completed painting offers insight into your emotional distribution—perhaps showing concentrated intensity in certain areas while others remain unmarked, or revealing unexpected juxtapositions between seemingly contradictory feelings coexisting within your physical form.

Try Painting Emotional Dialogues

This exercise explores how different emotions interact with each other through visual conversation. Select two distinctly different feelings currently present in your experience—perhaps vulnerability and strength, grief and gratitude, anxiety and curiosity, or any pair that seems to exist in a relationship within you.

Assign each emotion a different color palette. Begin painting with one emotion, allowing its quality to determine not just color but also shape, line quality, texture, and composition. After establishing its presence on one side or area of the canvas, begin introducing the second emotion in its designated colors and qualities.

Watch what happens as these emotional energies meet on the canvas. Do they remain separate? Create boundaries between themselves? Blend and transform each other? Fight for dominance? Dance together in unexpected harmony? Let the painting process reveal the natural relationship between these feeling states without forcing a predetermined outcome.

This visual dialogue often illuminates relationships between emotions that logical thinking cannot grasp, revealing how seemingly opposing feelings might actually nourish and complete each other when allowed to interact authentically.

Try Painting Emotional Memory Landscapes

Select a significant emotional memory—one that still carries energetic charge when recalled. Close your eyes and revisit this memory not through narrative detail but through sensory and emotional qualities. What colors, textures, shapes, and movements characterize this remembered experience?

Create an abstract landscape that captures the emotional topography of this memory. Perhaps a childhood joy becomes rolling hills in summer light; perhaps a profound loss manifests as a deep ravine with shadowed depths; perhaps a transformative insight appears as a path opening through a previously impenetrable forest.

This approach allows emotional memories to exist as landscapes rather than stories, freeing them from linear narrative and revealing their spatial, textural, and atmospheric qualities. The completed painting offers not illustration but emotional essence—the felt sense that remains when specific details have faded.

Creativity as the Key to an Extraordinary Life

To live extraordinarily means to inhabit the full spectrum of human feeling, allowing emotions to flow through us not as interruptions to normal functioning but as the essential current that animates our existence. When we learn to channel this emotional energy into creative expression, we discover that every feeling—even those culturally labeled as negative or problematic—contains seeds of insight, connection, and transformation.

Creative expression provides meaning by translating abstract internal experience into concrete external form. A moment of overwhelming grief captured in a charcoal drawing doesn't diminish the feeling's intensity but gives it purpose—transforming private suffering into shared human experience. The act of creation doesn't erase difficult emotions but integrates them into a larger context where they become not just bearable but valuable.

Art turns pain into power through the alchemical process of conscious transformation. The painter who faces their deepest fear by giving it visual form discovers that externalization creates crucial distance—the feeling remains real but no longer all-encompassing. What once existed as a formless threat becomes a defined entity, something that can be witnessed, explored, and ultimately understood as messenger rather than enemy.

Creativity expands emotional intelligence through continuous practice in recognizing, naming, and expressing subtle feeling states. The artist develops fluency in emotional language—learning to distinguish between similar but distinct experiences like disappointment and disillusionment, contentment and joy, anxiety and excitement. This refined perception enriches not just artistic work but every relationship and life decision.

Expression fosters connection by creating bridges between individual experience and collective understanding. When we transform personal emotions into art—whether shared publicly or kept private—we participate in the great human conversation about what it means to exist in vulnerable, feeling bodies on this earth. Even the most solitary creative act connects us to the universal human struggle to make meaning from the raw material of emotional experience.

A creative life becomes a fully lived life through the continuous practice of presence with whatever arises. The artist learns that every emotional state—from ecstatic joy to profound grief, from burning anger to quiet contentment—offers unique gifts when approached with curiosity rather than judgment. This openness to the complete spectrum of human feeling creates a life characterized not by perpetual happiness but by depth, authenticity, and the profound satisfaction of full engagement.

The Invitation: Embrace, Create, Transform

The canvas awaits. The page remains blank. The instrument sits silent. The body stands still. Each creative medium offers itself as a vessel for the transformation of formless feeling into tangible expression—not to capture emotions as static artifacts but to participate in their natural movement from internal experience to external form and back again in endless dialogue.

Every emotion carries creative potential: anger's fierce energy, grief's profound depth, joy's expansive light, fear's heightened awareness, peace's spacious clarity. None need be rejected or privileged above others. All belong in the complete palette of human experience, offering their particular qualities to the ongoing creation of a life fully lived.

The extraordinary life emerges not from avoiding emotional intensity but from engaging it directly through creative practice. Each brushstroke, each written word, each musical phrase, each movement becomes both question and response in the continuous conversation between our inner and outer worlds—the living dialogue that transforms mere existence into authentic, meaningful participation in the mysterious unfolding.

Let this spark a personal invitation to engage in some of the materials and suggestions set forth in this book. Make sure to read the section on Whitestone's Wanderlust program toward the end of this book to get more insights on how the human psyche works and ways to foster your own inner resources of wholeness that can supercharge your awareness around the parts of the mind that keep us resisting the more creative road ahead.

Folly of War

Shut your eyes, put your hand on your belly, breathe deeply. In this region of the body, what do you feel? Emptiness, discomfort, warmth, or satisfaction?

Folly of War

When I squeezed those paint bottles over this canvas, I wasn't just making art—I was screaming a question that kept me up at night: Why are we still doing this? I remember watching the news about Ukraine and Russia, feeling that weird mix of anger and helplessness. You know that feeling? When something terrible is happening but you're just sitting there with a paintbrush? So I decided to let my hands say what my words couldn't. See that angel-like shape emerging from the dark background? I used the colors of Ukraine, Russia, and America deliberately—because in war, everyone thinks they have angels on their side. But angels shouldn't have to pick teams.

The airplane dropping butter instead of bombs came from this crazy thought I had: What if all the money, all the energy, all the genius that goes into making weapons went into something ridiculous but harmless instead? Like butter. Tons of butter dropped from planes would make a huge mess. People would get stuck. We'd spend years cleaning it up. We'd complain. But we'd be alive to complain. That chaotic splash in the lower right with "R.I.P."? That's the aftermath of all our choices. The chaos we create when we let our inner demons drive our actions.

But maybe peace isn't something that happens between countries first. Maybe it has to start inside each person—one heart figuring out how to quiet its own shadows, one mind learning to question its need for enemies. I don't know if this painting changes anything. But for the few hours I worked on it, it changed me. It gave my frustration somewhere to go besides inward. And maybe that's a tiny start—one more person imagining a world where we drop butter instead of bombs, where we make messes we can clean up together instead of destruction we can never repair.

What would you drop from planes if you could replace all the world's bombs with something else? Scan the QR code to see the painting change.

Sacral Response

Broken? That's how the light gets in.

When I first learned about my human design, I discovered something amazing about my broken pieces. I'd been making choices from my wild monkey mind instead of listening to my body's wisdom. Now, I pause when emotions flood in. I wait until I feel that true "yes" or "no" in my belly. It turns out my body knows things my racing thoughts can't grasp. For so long, I felt scattered and fragmented, ignoring the signals my body sent. But now I see my cracks differently—like sunlight hitting broken glass and sending rainbows dancing across the walls.

Fortune Fish

Take a walk in nature, find a quiet resting place, and smell everything. How do you express smell without using words?

Fortune Fish

When I painted "Fortune Fish," I was trying to capture the feeling of being immersed in possibility. It's not just about how they look! Inside each fish is an inspiring fortune cookie message, inviting us to participate in life in ways that welcome serendipity.

The bright orange background is like when sunshine hits your closed eyelids and everything turns warm and glowy. Those textured patterns across the painting represent moments of revelation—some profound, some gentle—as you encounter unexpected wisdom.

The swirling coral-colored patterns show how inspiration doesn't just enter your mind—it ripples through your entire being and changes your entire rhythm. Have you ever noticed how your whole body seems to respond when you receive exactly the right message at the right time? You breathe differently, more fully.

I added those blue centers within each fish because even though good fortune often feels warm and welcoming, there's this surprising clarity that comes with it. It's like discovering a cool, shaded sanctuary exactly when you need it most.

What fascinates me is how encountering these fortune fish isn't just about reading messages—it transforms your internal state and even alters your perception of time. When I paint these creatures, I'm not trying to show just their appearance, but what it feels like to be in their presence, to receive their gifts, to let their wisdom transform you from the inside out.

Scan the QR Code to see the fish pop.

Breath Connection

I found communion in the space between breathing out and breathing in. Sitting by the pond watching dragonflies, I paid attention to my breath—especially that quiet moment after exhaling, before inhaling begins. That tiny pause felt important, like a secret doorway. Many spiritual traditions teach that this space between breaths connects us to something bigger than ourselves. The whole world seems to breathe—oceans with tides, trees taking in and releasing air, even mountains slowly rising and falling over millions of years. In that sacred pause between my own breaths, I felt linked to everything else that breathes. I wasn't separate from the dragonflies or pond or sky—we were all taking part in the same great inhale and exhale. Now, when I feel lonely or disconnected, I focus on that special space between breaths, remembering how it joins me to the breathing rhythm of all living things.

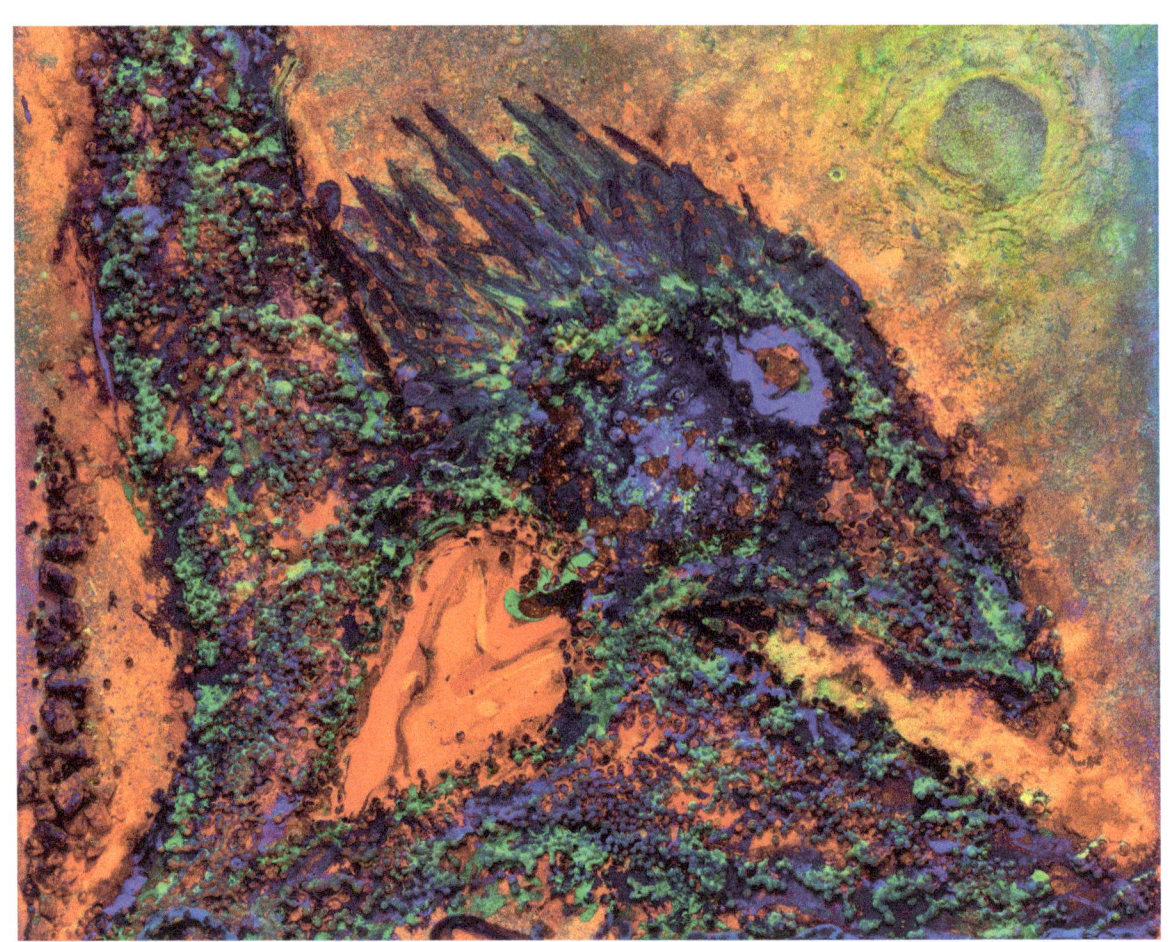

Sedona Glow Bird

How does it feel to be grounded in silence? Do you know how to fly with it?

Sedona Glow Bird

The "Sedona Glow Bird" explodes with the colors of desert evening skies. The vibrant coral backdrop emerged first, capturing the exact moment when Sedona's red rocks absorb the day's final light and radiate it back as their own luminous offering.

The bird materialized not through deliberate planning but through recognition, as if it had been waiting within the canvas for my hands to acknowledge its presence. I worked with fluorescent pigments that transform under black light, allowing this creature to exist simultaneously in multiple realities—one visible in ordinary light, another revealed in darkness.

Those tiny beads scattered across the bird's form represent love's unexpected appearances, birthed from the heart of the bird herself. Each bead catches and holds light differently, just as love manifests uniquely depending on how we're positioned to receive it. The distant sun provides the energetic pull necessary for the bird's emergence and flight. It creates the gravitational balance that makes flight possible, offering both destination and origin. There's an emotional tension in how the bird presses against the canvas edges—as if at any moment it could fly off the canvas to hug the viewer. The unconscious opening of arms, a slight lifting of the chest, a physical remembering of what it means to transcend limitation. The question isn't whether we want to fly, but whether we'll recognize when we're already soaring.

Heartbeat Silence in Flight

Between heartbeats, I discovered silence is Earth's original prayer. Put your hand on your chest and feel your heartbeat. Thump ... (silence) ... thump ... (silence). There's a quiet moment between each beat. I never noticed this until I immersed myself in the canyons of Capitol Reef, UT. Standing in a softly flowing river, cutting its way through the massive red mesa, I felt the space between my heartbeats. I felt connected to everything—the trees, rocks, especially the hundreds of birds swirling in the fresh mountain air. It was like the whole world was taking a tiny breath together in that open silent space. Native Americans called this "the space where the Creator lives." I think silence was the Earth's first way of talking to the sky, a wisdom that only birds embody—like a prayer that doesn't need words. When things get noisy and confusing, I remember those spaces between my heartbeats and the birds mastering the breeze, where everything is quiet and perfect, just for a split second.

The Web of Life

Everything has a beginning, middle, and end. Where are you right now on your journey? Are you prepared for the end? Did you fulfill your most creative, authentic self?

The Web of Life

"The Web of Life" speaks to how everything in existence forms an intricate, interconnected pattern. The vibrant background color and concentric circles weren't planned but seemed to create a ripples-on-water effect, tree rings, sound waves, planetary orbits. I placed the spiders, living creatures, in these perfect geometric formations, showing how nature creates extraordinary structure from almost nothing.

The nine glow stones are like guardians of the web. Each one glows with its cool light, like moments of clarity within the larger mystery. I placed these stones intuitively at points where the circular lines intersect, marking where different life paths cross and create opportunities for transformation.

A spider's circular web is among nature's most efficient designs—strong enough to withstand winds, flexible enough to bend without breaking, precise enough to catch exactly what's needed for sustenance. What fascinates me is how spiders rebuild their webs daily—a reminder that these patterns of connection require constant renewal and attention. The nine glowing points invite viewers to recognize their position within larger webs of connection—where are you on this intricate pattern? Which luminous node represents your current journey? The painting asks us to consider not just our individual path but our place within the greater circle of life.

Spiral Dance

My spiral trust continues to enfold as I learned to integrate the spiral dance that seems to circle yet always moves deeper. When I first hiked the mountain trail, I got frustrated with all the switchbacks. "Can't we just go straight up?" I complained. But later, looking at fossils in the rock wall, I noticed spiral patterns everywhere in nature—from snail shells to unfurling ferns, from whirlpools to galaxies spinning in space. These spirals weren't going in circles—they were growing outward or inward through a beautiful pattern. My own life follows this shape. Sometimes I feel like I'm facing the same problems again and again, but really, I'm meeting them at a different level each time, like climbing a spiral staircase. When I stopped fighting the spiral path and started dancing with it, moving with its natural flow, each curve brought new discoveries. Now I trust life's spiral wisdom, knowing even when I seem to circle back, I'm actually traveling deeper.

Gratitude Glow Garden

Take time to follow your grief, you may find a new surprise waiting on the other side. Do you know how to take a grief walk? (see Wanderlust Section in the book for directive)

Gratitude Glow Garden

When I first started painting this, I had no idea these smiley faces would show up! That's one of my favorite things about creating—sometimes your hands know things before your brain does. I called it "Gratitude Glow Garden" because even though these faces looked kind of spooky, they made me feel thankful. Weird, right? But here's the thing—these little demons weren't scary to me at all. They felt like old friends.

For years, I'd carried these "demons" inside me. You know those voices that tell you to be careful? The ones that say, "Don't try that," or, "What if you mess up?" I used to think they were my enemies, holding me back. But as I painted, I realized they were just trying to keep me safe all along. The bright greens and oranges brought forth a feeling that a safe garden might bring, like the feeling when you finally understand something that has confused you forever. It's like your heart goes, "Ohhhh!" and suddenly lights up with all these colors. Scan the QR code to see how it glows. Scan the QR code to see the garden glow.

Making friends with your inner demons is kind of like finally talking to the scary kid at school and finding out they're actually super nice. These faces aren't haunting me anymore—they're helping me grow. Sometimes I'm just a beautifully spooky garden variety human being, on fire for full immersion. This painting taught me that loving yourself means loving *all* the parts—even the weird, spooky ones that make you uncomfortable sometimes. They're all there for a reason.

Broken Branch Homes

I found kinship with broken branches still offering nests to birds. After the big windstorm, many tree branches in the park were cracked or broken. But they didn't fall off—they hung on, growing at odd angles. The cool thing was, birds still built nests in those broken branches. One maple tree had a branch practically upside down, but a robin family made it home anyway. I felt like those branches sometimes. Parts of me were broken by hard experiences, and I didn't grow in the "right" direction anymore. But those broken places in me could still be useful and beautiful. They could still hold precious things. Watching a mother bird feed her babies in a nest on a lightning-struck tree helped me see that being broken doesn't mean being worthless. Sometimes our cracks and weird angles make us better homes for love than if we'd stayed perfectly straight and unharmed. What parts of yourself have you been scared of that might actually be trying to help you? Do you want a mentor like Whitestone to show you how to embrace your demons?

Sweet Darkness

Do you explore the darkness within meditation practice, bringing your deep curiosity to your dark inner space? Try it. Record what you find daily.

Sweet Darkness

"Sweet Darkness" on black canvas was a true experiment in bringing a special glow to the painting. This deliberate embrace of darkness as foundation rather than absence became the perfect metaphor for how creativity often emerges most powerfully from void and mystery.

Those radiant light-green starburst formations emerged first with fluorescent paints under blacklight. The smaller coral-red bursts ended up creating visual rhythm and conversation between warm and cool luminosity. These fiery accents created a cosmic quality that mirrored the universe in all its starlit glory.

I love my glow stones, and here I found the perfect creation to use them as anchors to its surrounding explosion of glow paint, providing stability within expansion.

The painting's title emerged from my extensive exploration of dark places in the wilderness with the art of night wandering. The black background doesn't merely frame the glowing bursts but actively participates in their creation, revealing how limitation often catalyzes expression rather than constraining it. Scan the QR code to watch this one explode without light.

Darkness: A Training Ground

I learned to trust darkness as a patient teacher of inner sight. I set out, blind folded, with a drum far off in the distance. I was asked to move in the darkness through a wooded forest only using my hands to protect myself from walking into a large tree. Almost crawling on my knees, with hands extended in front of me and the expectation that I would bounce from the tree barrier, I actually made it to the drum, removed my blindfold, and turned to look where I had started. With amazement, I saw there was a forest of trees, each about four feet apart. I didn't even touch a single tree. This is where I discovered the sweet darkness. I found inner resources, even without sight, to navigate the wooded terrain. Darkness taught me to see in new ways. It's the same with sad or confusing times in life. When things feel dark and I can't figure stuff out, I've learned to be patient and wait. If I don't panic and run around, my heart learns to "see" things that my eyes miss. Darkness isn't always scary—sometimes it's just teaching us to find our way using different senses we forget about when all the lights are on.

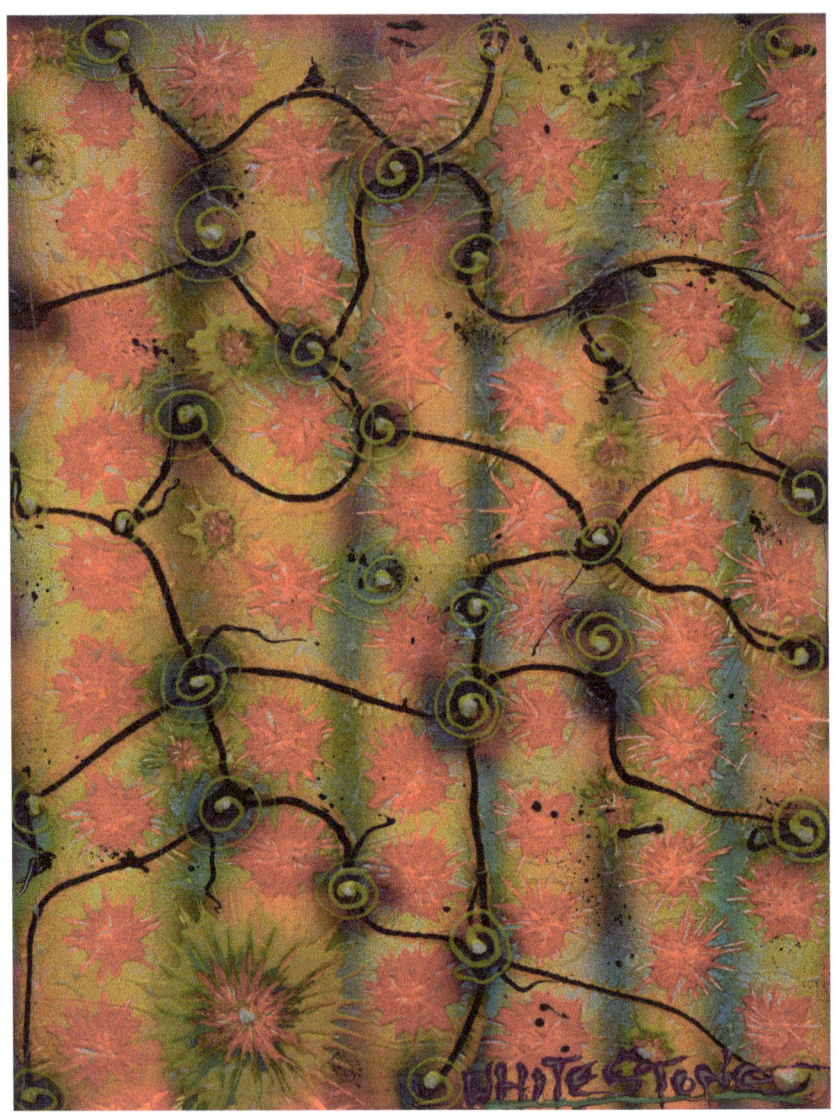

The Wild and the Wonderful

Where do you feel a deep connection? Do you go there often for life support?

The Wild and the Wonderful

I created "The Wild and the Wonderful" during a period when the borders between my interior landscape and the natural world began to dissolve. That golden-amber background appeared first—the exact color of late afternoon sunlight filtering through the forest canopy, that magical hour when everything ordinary suddenly reveals its extraordinary nature. It's like how flowers, snowflakes, and spider webs all speak the same mathematical language across completely different forms. The black spiraling pathways connecting these bursts of energy materialized as I contemplated the invisible networks that bind all living things, like how mycelium threads connect entire forests underground, how birds follow ancient migratory pathways mapped in their genetic memory, how water cycles from ocean to cloud to rain to river and back again.

Under normal light, this painting shows one reality—the visible connections we can easily name and recognize. But when darkness falls and the fluorescent elements begin to glow, another dimension reveals itself. This dual nature reminds us that we're never truly alone, even in our darkest moments. The glowing version speaks to how nature continues its conversation even when human attention turns elsewhere. This painting invites us to remember our place within these ancient, ongoing conversations—not as observers but as participants in a wild and wonderful network of relationship that never ceases, whether we're conscious of it or not. Scan the QR code to see it change.

Empty Canvas

The wilderness taught me that emptiness is not absence but invitation—white canvas awaiting the trembling brush of being. Standing in the wide desert for the first time, I felt scared by all that open space—nothing to hide behind. No distractions. Just vast, empty landscape stretching forever. But as I stood quietly, that emptiness began feeling different—not like something missing but like something waiting. Artists know this about blank canvases—they're not empty in a sad way but in an excited, anything-could-happen way! The desert's beautiful emptiness invited me to be truly present without hiding behind busyness or noise. Once I settled in, I began to see how the cactus had thorns to protect itself, and I began thinking about how they store so much water for life support. I began seeing how everything was connected in a beautiful chaotic flow. Now, when I face empty pages or quiet days or unknown futures, I feel that same desert invitation: this is not absence of fear but open space where new life waits to emerge through my trembling, truth-seeking heart.

PART SEVEN

110 Emotions to Make You Crazy or Bring New Life

> "The truest and most moving landscapes of human emotion are mapped across our faces, sculpted through our actions, and painted on the canvas of our relationships. Any artist who learns to navigate these hundred emotional territories—with their treacherous ravines and unexpected vistas—discovers that life's masterpiece lies not in avoiding complexity but in embracing it with the curious heart of an explorer." —Maya Angelou

Across the vast terrain of human experience, a hundred emotions bloom like wildflowers after rain—some brilliant and demanding our attention, others subtle and easily overlooked, many growing entangled at their roots. To navigate this wilderness of feeling is to embark on the most profound adventure of existence—learning that joy's summit appears more magnificent for having traversed sorrow's valley, that courage blossoms from fear's fertile soil, that peace emerges not from emotional absence but from embracing the complete spectrum with open arms. In this intricate emotional ecosystem, we discover that life's richness dwells not in avoiding storms but in dancing within them, gathering wisdom from each passing weather until we recognize that our capacity to feel deeply—in all directions—is not our burden but our birthright, our most exquisite gift.

110 Emotions

Primary Positive Emotions
1. Joy
2. Happiness
3. Contentment
4. Satisfaction
5. Pride
6. Admiration
7. Love
8. Affection

9. Gratitude
10. Enthusiasm
11. Amusement
12. Excitement
13. Hope
14. Relief
15. Optimism
16. Serenity
17. Inspiration
18. Awe
19. Confidence
20. Trust
21. Empathy
22. Compassion
23. Curiosity
24. Encouragement
25. Warmth

Primary Negative Emotions
26. Sadness
27. Grief
28. Disappointment
29. Regret
30. Loneliness
31. Hopelessness
32. Despair
33. Depression
34. Guilt
35. Shame
36. Embarrassment
37. Frustration
38. Annoyance
39. Anger
40. Resentment
41. Disgust
42. Contempt
43. Hatred
44. Envy
45. Jealousy
46. Anxiety

47. Fear
48. Dread
49. Worry
50. Nervousness

Mixed and Complex Emotions
51. Nostalgia (happiness + sadness)
52. Bittersweetness (joy + sadness)
53. Love with longing (affection + sadness)
54. Schadenfreude (joy + maliciousness)
55. Guilty pleasure (enjoyment + guilt)
56. Surprise (neutral, but often mixed with fear or joy)
57. Relief (joy + previous fear)
58. Gratification (joy + satisfaction)
59. Awe (wonder + admiration + fear)
60. Betrayal (anger + sadness)
61. Insecurity (fear + self-doubt)
62. Hopefulness (optimism + uncertainty)
63. Alienation (sadness + disconnection)
64. Vindication (relief + resentment)
65. Anticipation (excitement + uncertainty)

Low-Intensity Emotions
66. Calmness
67. Relaxation
68. Mild amusement
69. Light curiosity
70. Slight disappointment
71. Mild irritation
72. Subtle concern
73. Gentle affection
74. Soft admiration
75. Quiet determination
76. Ecstasy (intense joy)
77. Rage (intense anger)
78. Terror (intense fear)
79. Deep despair (intense sadness)
80. Overwhelming gratitude
81. Exhilaration (intense excitement)
82. Deep humiliation

83. Intense longing
84. Overpowering awe
85. Utter hopelessness

High-Intensity Emotions
86. Ecstasy (intense joy)
87. Rage (intense anger)
88. Terror (intense fear)
89. Deep despair (intense sadness)
90. Overwhelming gratitude
91. Exhilaration (intense excitement)
92. Deep humiliation
93. Intense longing
94. Overpowering awe
95. Utter hopelessness

Social and Moral Emotions
96. Righteous indignation (anger + moral belief)
97. Social embarrassment (shame in public)
98. Moral disgust (disapproval + disgust)
99. Compassionate sorrow (sadness for others)
100. Protective instinct (love + fear for another's safety)
101. Remorse (guilt + regret)
102. Inferiority (shame + insecurity)
103. Outrage (anger + moral violation)
104. Feeling wronged (resentment + victimization)
105. Defensive pride (pride + insecurity)

Situational and Transient Emotions
106. Startle (quick surprise + fear)
107. Hesitation (uncertainty + caution)
108. Confusion (uncertainty + frustration)
109. Empowerment (confidence + control)
110. Surrender (acceptance + giving up)

Emotion Reflection Journal
Exploring the Depth of Your Emotions
Each day, choose one emotion from this book and use the reflective questions below to explore its role in your life. The goal is to embrace each emotion as a way to find a deeper loving voice

from within that can ignite a more imaginative and creative way to live your life. Write freely and honestly. As mentioned in Part One of this book, don't avoid working your journal with some of the more challenging emotions that you might be avoiding. If we don't embrace the more challenging or darker emotions, we may be missing out on their important role in expanding our imagination and our willingness to explore the things that might be calling us to deeper discovery.

Unleash Your Wild Emotional Self:

Each emotion carries **wisdom**—whether it's joy showing what fulfills you, or fear highlighting what needs care. Approach each emotion with curiosity rather than judgment. Let this journal be a guide to transforming your emotional world into deeper **self-awareness and creative intelligence.** Make your goal in this journaling a tool to ignite your imagination.

Journal Prompt:

1. Describe a moment when you recently felt this emotion. What triggered it?
2. How does this emotion show up in your body (e.g., tension, warmth, heaviness, lightness)?
3. What thoughts accompanied this emotion? Were they helpful or limiting?
4. How did this emotion influence your actions or decisions? Use one or two current specific examples. Did it empower you or hold you back?
5. What patterns do you notice? Does this emotion arise often in similar situations? How can you embrace this emotion as a way to love yourself or forgive yourself?
6. How does this emotion affect your relationships, goals, and overall well-being?
7. If this emotion could speak, what would it tell you?
8. How can you harness or regulate this emotion in a healthy way?
9. What does this emotion reveal about what truly matters to you?
10. What creative endeavor can you explore or continue to foster as an honest reflection of your life experience?
11. How can you become an emotional channel for others?
12. How can you offer publicly or use social media to offer your new emotional awareness as a gift to the world?
13. How can you hold your emotional life as sacred? How can you hold more space for others to explore their emotional life?

Continue to the back of this book to get more insights on creative coaching, books, workshops, intensives, and resources to support the exciting journey ahead.

The Gift of Light

How do you feel about wearing more color? What feelings come out when you wear something that attracts an emotional response from others?

The Gift of Light

When I painted these starbursts, I was thinking about Christmas lights—you know how they make even ordinary living rooms feel magical? But then I realized stars aren't just for December. They're always up there, always glowing, whether we look up or not.

I painted some stars with spirals in the middle because I believe light doesn't just shine outward, it also pulls us inward, making us think about stuff that matters—like how each morning is basically Earth giving us a brand-new canvas to create on.

The colors glow extra bright under black light, which reminds me that sometimes we need different perspectives to see the magic that's been there all along. Things that seem ordinary in regular light become amazing when you change how you look at them.

I called it "The Gift of Light" because light is something we're given every day, not just during holidays. The sun rising is basically the universe saying, "Here's another chance to make something awesome today."

What lights up your world on ordinary days? What stars do you follow when things get dark?

Twilight Shadows

At twilight's threshold, I discovered how shadows hold the memory of light. At sunset by the lake, I watched how darkness gradually replaced brightness. But something magical happened in between—the shadows weren't just absent of light, they were purple and deep blue, holding the day's golden warmth within their darkness. They remembered the light even as it departed. This helped me understand sad times in a new way. When happiness fades and darker feelings come, they still contain traces of joy within them. The outline of what's gone remains visible in what's present. Native people honor twilight as sacred time—not day, not night, but the mysterious in-between where both exist together. I started sitting outside during this "between time," watching how everything transforms. Now, when I feel myself moving from one emotional season to another, I pay attention to the beautiful shadow-colors created in the transition, knowing they hold memories of what came before.

After The Storm

Try following your breath and see where it takes you?

After The Storm

I painted "After The Storm" on a day when the wind wasn't just something I felt—it was something I became. Have you ever stood somewhere so wild that you forgot where your body ended and the world began? That's what happened on that coastal bluff, with the Pacific stretching endlessly before me.

The diagonal streaks across this canvas seemed to have the same rhythm as the wind carving through everything around me that day. I stopped thinking and started breathing—really breathing. The yellow sun/moon was something I felt rising inside me as I sat there. It's weird how sometimes the brightest things come alive in us when we're facing something powerful and wild, isn't it? The fluorescent paints let me capture something regular colors couldn't. With the lights out, the painting takes a comforting while eerie effect.

This painting reminds me that being alive is all about breathing. It's about letting yourself be carved by experiences, letting winds of change move through you instead of fighting them. Sometimes we need to eat the wind—to take in something wild and powerful—before we can make something colorful from inside ourselves. Scan the QR code to see wild nature moving in the dark.

Breath Spaces

I discovered how to paint the space between breaths—that spiritual pause where transformation dwells. Sitting very still in my backyard, I noticed something about breathing I'd never noticed before. Between breathing out and breathing in, there's a tiny, quiet moment of perfect stillness. It's not empty waiting. I wanted to capture this special in-between space in my painting. Not the inhale or exhale, but the sacred pause between them where change happens. Using soft colors that blended at the edges, I tried painting not the objects themselves but the spaces where they touched each other—where sky meets mountain, where water meets shore. These boundary places buzzed with a special energy I could feel but not explain. I now notice that quiet space between my breaths, honoring it as the magical workshop where life remakes itself moment by moment.

Aloha

Upon awakening, how can you shift consciousness by reflecting on the mystery of the new day? Can you embrace the unknown as an invitation into letting go?

Aloha

When I painted "Aloha," I wanted to capture that feeling when you wake up and realize the day could be amazing. You know that feeling? Like when you're half-asleep but already smiling?

Those yellow sunbursts didn't start as flowers or stars—they started as feelings. I mixed bright yellows and reds because that's what joy feels like inside my chest—warm and buzzing with energy. Each one is like a little explosion of "hello" bursting out from the inside. Those tiny black marks scattered throughout? Those are the little surprises in life—the unexpected texts from friends, finding money in your pocket, or that perfect song coming on exactly when you need it. I didn't plan where they would go—I just let them find their own places. I painted this to remind myself (and now you!) that magic isn't something we have to go looking for. It's already inside us, just waiting for us to say, "Aloha," to it. When we welcome each day as a gift that's happening *for* us, not *to* us, everything starts to look brighter.

What would your "hello" to the world look like if you painted it today? What colors would you choose to show how your heart feels when it's most alive?

Star Stories

The stars whispered ancient stories through my dreams when I surrendered to darkness. Scared of the dark as a kid, I kept night-lights burning. But camping far from city lights, I had no choice but to face the night. Lying in my sleeping bag, the immense starry sky overwhelming me, I finally stopped fighting darkness and simply let it be. That night, dreams came like I'd never experienced—vivid stories that seemed to come from the stars themselves. Many cultures believe stars speak to us when we sleep beneath them. The Greeks saw constellations as myths written in light; Aboriginal Australians call the Milky Way "the dreaming track." When I stopped pushing away darkness with artificial brightness, these cosmic stories found me again. Now I sometimes turn off all lights and sit in peaceful darkness, allowing night to rewrap me in its original embrace. In surrendering to what I feared, I reconnected with the universe's oldest bedtime stories, whispered in starlight.

Imagine

The world needs your imagination as much as you do to feel your true purpose.

Imagine

I painted "Imagine" on one of those days when my heart felt too big for my body. You know that feeling? The sunset colors came first—those warm oranges and pinks that remind you anything is possible. Have you ever watched the sky during sunset and felt like the world was trying to tell you something important? That's what these colors whisper to me. Look closely and see the hidden messages in the painting.

When I added the glow paint (which you can't fully see in this photo), something amazing happened. The painting started living two different lives—one in regular light and another in darkness. Isn't that exactly what imagination does? It shows us what others might not see, revealing hidden magic in ordinary things.

The swirly lavender and black ground beneath the circle feels like the place where ideas first bubble up—messy, mysterious, and beautiful all at once. Sometimes our best creations come from chaos, from letting our hands play before our brains can tell them, "That's not right."

When I turn off the lights and this painting glows, it reminds me that our imaginations never really shut off. They're always shining, even when the world around us goes dark. Maybe that's why I love painting with glow effects so much—they're like dreams you can see with your eyes wide open. Scan the QR code to see how the sun can change into a setting moon over the ocean.

Bone Memory

My bones remember what my mind forgot about belonging to this world. Reading books and using computers made me think humans were separate from nature. Every day I was losing touch with my imagination by spending hours scrolling and pondering how others seemed to be more creative than I. But when I arrived at Aravaipa Canyon Ranch , I felt my bones relax, like the feeling of water—like they remembered something from my childhood innocence. Science says our bodies are made of the same elements as stars and soil. My bones know this truth, even when my busy brain forgets. When I'm quiet enough, I can feel my skeleton humming with a feeling of returning home. My marrow remembers being part of everything. This belonging lives deep in the oldest parts of me, waiting for quiet moments to whisper, "You have always been home."

SOAR

How do birds make you feel there is more to life than what you think?

SOAR

I painted "SOAR" during a day when I felt stuck inside my own thoughts, like I was trapped in a room with no windows. You know that feeling? When your brain keeps spinning the same tired stories over and over? Scan the QR Code to see the birds take night flight.

That fiery orange background came first—it just poured out of me like my hands were trying to create sunrise inside my studio. Sometimes the most honest colors come when we stop thinking and just let our feelings pick up the brush.

The birds weren't planned. They showed up on their own—that purple one on the left appeared first, almost like it was peeking around the corner to check if it was safe to come out. Have you ever noticed how birds never seem worried about whether they're "good enough" at flying? They just spread their wings and trust the air to hold them.

I splashed those blue streaks across the middle when I remembered something important: birds don't just fly because they have wings—they fly because they have hollow bones. They're light inside. Sometimes we need to empty ourselves of heavy thoughts before we can rise.

The lime-green bird on the right side has always been my favorite part of this painting. It looks like it's just realized it can fly, like it's having that "oh!" moment we all get when we suddenly understand something that seemed impossible.

What I love about painting birds is that they remind me I don't have to fly all the time. They spend plenty of time on branches, on the ground, building nests. They know when to soar and when to rest. Maybe that's the real wisdom they're always trying to share with us.

New Songs Rising

I found my voice in the space where broken things sing their truth. I remember the old wind chime that fell and got bent. Dad hung it up anyway, and it made different sounds—not what it was supposed to, but something new and interesting. That's how I found my real voice. When I stopped trying to sound perfect like everyone expected—when I let my voice crack or show the rough edges of how I really felt—that's when people actually started listening to me. There's a special kind of music that only broken things can make. The Japanese fix broken pottery with gold to show that the breaks are valuable parts of the story. My most honest words come from the cracked places in my heart—that's where my truth lives, singing its strange, beautiful song.

Forest on Fire

Write down something you need to give up, say a prayer, then throw it into a fire and trust transformation as essential for moving on.

Forest on Fire

I painted "Forest On Fire" during a time when big changes were sweeping through my life like wildfire. Have you ever felt something ending and beginning at the exact same time? That's what inspired this painting.

The swirling reds, oranges, and golds came first—colors that feel hot and alive when they flow from your brush. I used glow paints because fire isn't just one thing—it changes how it looks depending on whether you're seeing it in daylight or darkness. Scan the QR code to watch the fire spread with light.

I waited until these bright colors dried before adding the black tree shapes with a simple black marker. Sometimes the most important parts of our stories are the simplest ones. These trees aren't detailed or fancy—they're just honest outlines standing in the middle of all that color and heat.

Fire has always fascinated me because it's the perfect teacher about change. It can be gentle enough to warm your hands or wild enough to transform an entire forest. It doesn't ask permission—it just does what fire does.

The question this painting asks me (and maybe you too) is whether I'll use the fires in my life to create warmth and light, or if I'll ignore them until they grow too big to control. Will I invite transformation in small, meaningful ways, or will I resist until change forces its way through anyway?

What's amazing about forests is that they already know the answer. After the fire passes through, they don't waste time with regret. They just begin again, sending up new green shoots through the ashes, turning darkness into the exact nutrients needed for new growth.

Path in Ruins

When did you realize nothing lasts forever, that there is a beginning, middle, and end to everything and every relationship? When loss became a reality in my life, I felt scared at first. Where would I walk now? But in surrender, I felt the desire to move forward to embrace something new that seemed to always emerge from the ashes of grief. Sometimes things must burn away and fall apart before we can see the cool rising path hiding underneath. The lost and broken parts weren't garbage—they were like puzzle pieces showing me a secret way forward that I never would have found if everything had stayed perfect and neat.

Kake Walk

What brings you delight? How can you change to have more delight in your life?

Kake Walk

When I splashed these colors onto my canvas, I wasn't trying to be perfect. I wanted to capture how it feels when life is just … fun! You know those days when everything makes you smile? That's what I was feeling.

The bright oranges and reds burst out like laughter. The swirls and shapes dance around each other just like my thoughts do when I'm super excited. See those blue circles hiding in the corners? That's like those quiet moments when I take a breath before jumping back into the joy.

Sometimes people think art has to be serious or complicated. But this painting is my reminder that life can be a "Kake Walk"—easy and sweet—if we just let ourselves enjoy it. The messy parts, the bright parts, they're all mixed together because that's how emotions work.

When I painted this, I felt free. Free to make marks without worrying if they were "right." Free to let the colors crash into each other. That's the whole point—finding freedom in the chaos of fun.

What makes you feel this joy and be the change you want to see in the world?

River Memories

I developed so many great memories with rivers throughout the Southwest. The river is not just an incredible playground, but it's the perfect environment to remind myself that I need to get into the flow. When I'm in the flow, everything is fun, even work. That's been my goal over the last 40 years. How do I find the joy of being in the flow in everything I do? I believe we are here to have life and have it abundantly. It's a mindset as well as a discipline. I've had to take time out over and over to allow myself to reflect on the great mysteries of the natural world. I've had to learn how to embody the chaos of life and see that everything disappears in the reality that something new is being created. When I'm in the flow, life is a cakewalk.

Universal Whirlwind

The universe is expanding faster than we ever knew possible, so should our consciousness. What can you do to expand your universal mind?

Universal Whirlwind

Have you ever stared up at the night sky and felt super small but also like you're part of something huge? That's exactly how I felt while creating this swirling vortex of colors.

When I painted "Universal Whirlwind," I was thinking about how our minds are kind of like the universe—always growing, always spinning with new ideas. Those little spiky circles scattered throughout? I used oranges and yellows that blend into greens and blues because that's how expanding feels to me—warm and exciting at first, then cooling into something deeper as it grows. The spiral pulls you in, just like when you get really curious about something and can't stop thinking about it. Scan the QR code to see the universe expand with color.

Sometimes expanding our minds feels scary—like we might spin out of control. But I wanted this painting to show that it can also be beautiful and exciting! Each stroke of my brush was me saying, "I'm not afraid to grow bigger than I am right now."

The coolest part? Our minds can actually expand faster than the universe if we let them. A single thought can zoom across galaxies in seconds. That's the magic I was trying to capture—that dizzy, amazing feeling when your brain makes a connection that wasn't there before. What makes your mind feel like it's spinning with possibilities?

Void Creation

I learned that creation begins in the void between heartbeats, where silence gathers its courage. Pressing my ear against a wooden box, I heard heartbeats—my own, echoing back. I noticed something important: between each "lub-dub" was a tiny space of silence. That silent pause isn't empty waiting—it's where the next heartbeat gets ready to happen! Many creation stories from around the world describe how everything started from nothing—from empty space or silent darkness. Before the first word or light or creature came a sacred emptiness that held all possibilities. When I sit in the quiet moments between busy activities, not filling them with noise or screens, I can feel that same creative power gathering. Ideas that never would have found me in the noise suddenly appear. Scientists now say even outer space isn't really empty—it buzzes with invisible energy and possibility. When I honor the quiet spaces in my day, my heartbeat, my sentences, I'm making room for new things to be born from that ancient creative void.

PART EIGHT

It's Your Turn

"Create as if your soul is the canvas and time is running out—because in art, we don't just make things, we make ourselves immortal." —Georgia O'Keeffe

Emotion Reflection Journal Guide

Grab a journal or a painting pad and each day choose a question or bold statement from the art reflection pages of this book. What emotion does it evoke in the moment, and how can you expand on the invitation to create a unique reflection or picture of what arises in the moment?

Dive into creating art like you'd splash into a summer lake—with joyful abandon and zero apologies! The canvas or blank page doesn't care about perfection, only your willingness to play, experiment, and make magnificent messes. Remember: masterpieces begin as mistakes, breakthroughs arrive through blunders, and the most important skill isn't technique but the courage to start. Your creativity isn't some serious, sacred temple—it's a wild playground where your inner child finally gets permission to run free, paintbrush in hand, laughing at the sheer delight of making something from nothing. The world needs your particular brand of creative mischief, so jump in—the artistic waters are waiting, and they're warmer than you think.

Exploring the Depth of Your Emotions

Each morning arrives as uncharted territory, a landscape whose features remain hidden until explored through conscious presence. The questions that await in these reflection pages are not merely words but doorways—thresholds between the known self and the vast wilderness of possibility that stirs beneath familiar patterns of thought and feeling.

To choose one question, one bold statement each day, is to select a particular trailhead from which to begin your wandering. Some paths may lead through sun-dappled meadows of joyful recollection; others might traverse the shadowed valleys of grief or regret. Each terrain offers its particular wisdom, its unique perspective on the panorama of your becoming.

The reflective questions become walking sticks for this journey—tools that steady your steps as you navigate unfamiliar emotional topography. They invite you to pause at overlooks, to examine the layers of sediment that form your personal history, to notice how certain feelings create thermal updrafts that lift consciousness toward unexpected vistas of understanding.

When you find yourself standing before the blank page, the empty canvas, remember that creation begins not with certainty but with surrender. Allow the questions to dissolve the boundaries between thinking and feeling, between observation and expression. Let your hand become a divining rod, sensing the underground streams of emotion that flow beneath conscious awareness, drawing them upward into visible form.

The personal emotional story that emerges may begin as a trickle—hesitant, tentative, testing the contours of permission. Give it space to gather momentum. Watch how it carves its own channels through resistance, how it finds its way around boulders of fear or judgment, how it eventually creates its own meandering path toward some larger body of understanding.

Poetry arises when emotion distills into essential elements—when the vast weather system of feeling condenses into concentrated droplets of language. Begin with the bodily sensation of the emotion currently moving through you. Is it the fluttering wings of anxiety beneath your ribs? The heavy stone of grief in your belly? The warm sunlight of contentment spreading across your chest? Let these physical metaphors guide your first lines, trusting that the poem already exists within the feeling, waiting only for your willingness to follow its contours into language.

The drawing or painting emerges through similar attentiveness—not as an illustration of emotion but as its direct embodiment. Color becomes the visible spectrum of feeling; line quality translates emotional texture; composition reveals the relationship between various aspects of experience. The hand knows what the mind cannot yet articulate. Trust its intelligence as it transforms internal weather into external landscape.

The challenging emotions—those we instinctively avoid or suppress—contain particularly rich soil for creative exploration. Like forests after wildfire, these apparently desolate territories often harbor the most vigorous new growth. The anger that burns through pretense, the grief that softens hardened ground, the fear that heightens perception—these emotional intensities create conditions where imagination flourishes in unexpected forms.

Our avoidance of darker emotional territories reflects not their danger but their power. What we resist exploring often contains precisely the energy needed for transformation. The charcoal darkness of depression might hold the very pigment needed to create depth and dimension in your visual expression. The jagged rhythm of anxiety might provide the exact syncopation your poetic line requires. The chaotic swirl of confusion might contain the perfect storm system from which new understanding emerges.

Each day's exploration becomes another footstep in a larger pilgrimage—not toward some distant destination but into an ever-deepening presence with your own unfolding experience. The questions and statements from these reflection pages serve not as assignments to complete but as cairns marking possible routes through the wilderness of consciousness.

Remember that this journey requires no credentials, no particular skill beyond willingness. The most profound creative expressions often emerge not from technical mastery but from raw authenticity—from the courage to stand exposed in the full weather of your humanity and record what you discover there with whatever tools lie at hand.

The landscape awaits your footsteps. The page anticipates your voice. The canvas hungers for your particular vision. Begin where you are, with what you feel, trusting that each honest exploration creates not just external artifacts but internal passageways—new neural pathways through which life's current flows with greater freedom and resonance.

The imagination you seek already exists within you as seedling, as ember, as underground spring. Your creative practice becomes the seasonal attention that allows these latent potentials to emerge—the sunlight, the breath, the gentle disturbance of soil that transforms dormancy into vivid, visible life.

Unleash Your Wild Emotional Self

Each emotion carries **wisdom**—whether it's joy showing what fulfills you, or fear highlighting what needs care. Approach each emotion with curiosity rather than judgment. Let your painting/art form or journal be a guide to transforming your emotional world into deeper **self-awareness and creative intelligence.** Make your goal in this journaling a tool to ignite your imagination.

If you choose visual arts, here is a helpful guide in working with color. Please note that I would recommend going blind into an art store to buy color pens or paints and randomly start picking colors that are calling out to you. Later, you can explore the emotions that might be tied to those colors, providing insights to how you might be feeling. If you continue to be drawn to certain colors, this can provide some helpful information about your core comfort. I always recommend, as you continue an art practice, start choosing colors that make you uncomfortable.

Note, you can apply this to your wardrobe as well. Pushing yourself to wear more colorful clothes, while at first uncomfortable, may end up bringing you a more positive feeling about yourself, especially because people are drawn to colors, even though they may not allow themselves the freedom to wear them themselves. Once again, push yourself to show up differently once in a while.

The Color of Emotions

Here is a list of emotions with **two to three colors** that best represent each one. The colors are chosen based on **psychological associations, cultural interpretations, and visual symbolism** of emotions. Explore using colorful paints, pens, markers, or pencils for freeform sketching, painting, or drawing to explore how color can ignite your specific emotions.

Approach a blank canvas, or paper page with no expectation. Empty your mind and try to lose any particular image or idea that may come to your mind. Let the color lead the way, not the mind. If the mind takes over, that's okay too. No judgement, just go with the flow. Maybe try closing your eyes, moving to the colors you choose randomly across the blank page. After a few minutes of exploring this free-form activity, take the time to reflect on your creation. Try viewing it as if you were a five-year-old child. Take note of the feeling you have when finished. Take note of the feelings or thoughts that arise. Can you track them to the chapters in this book? Can you see how the experience is more important than the outcome?

Positive Emotions
1. **Joy** – Yellow, Gold, Bright Orange
2. **Happiness** – Sunshine Yellow, Warm Pink, Light Green
3. **Contentment** – Soft Blue, Sage Green, Warm Beige
4. **Satisfaction** – Deep Blue, Earthy Brown, Olive Green
5. **Pride** – Royal Purple, Deep Red, Gold
6. **Admiration** – Sky Blue, Soft Gold, Gentle Violet
7. **Love** – Deep Red, Soft Pink, Warm Peach
8. **Affection** – Blush Pink, Lavender, Light Coral
9. **Gratitude** – Warm Gold, Soft Green, Sunset Orange
10. **Enthusiasm** – Vibrant Orange, Bright Yellow, Electric Blue
11. **Amusement** – Playful Purple, Aqua Blue, Bright Yellow
12. **Excitement** – Neon Orange, Bright Red, Hot Pink
13. **Hope** – Soft Green, Light Yellow, Sky Blue
14. **Relief** – Pale Blue, Light Green, Muted Lavender
15. **Optimism** – Bright Yellow, Orange, Sky Blue
16. **Serenity** – Soft Blue, Light Lavender, Pale Green
17. **Inspiration** – Soft Gold, Light Blue, Violet
18. **Awe** – Deep Indigo, Silver, Midnight Blue
19. **Confidence** – Bold Blue, Fiery Red, Royal Gold
20. **Trust** – Deep Green, Navy Blue, Earthy Brown
21. **Empathy** – Soft Pink, Light Blue, Gentle Gray
22. **Compassion** – Warm Rose, Lavender, Pale Yellow
23. **Curiosity** – Bright Green, Teal, Light Orange
24. **Encouragement** – Bright Yellow, Warm Orange, Light Green
25. **Warmth** – Golden Yellow, Soft Orange, Peach

Negative Emotions
26. **Sadness** – Deep Blue, Gray, Muted Purple
27. **Grief** – Charcoal Gray, Deep Purple, Black
28. **Disappointment** – Dusty Blue, Faded Yellow, Muted Gray
29. **Regret** – Dark Green, Muted Brown, Grayish Blue
30. **Loneliness** – Pale Gray, Soft Purple, Deep Blue
31. **Hopelessness** – Dark Gray, Deep Purple, Muted Blue
32. **Despair** – Black, Deep Indigo, Shadowy Gray
33. **Depression** – Dark Blue, Deep Gray, Muted Purple

34. **Guilt** – Dark Red, Muted Brown, Shadow Gray
35. **Shame** – Deep Purple, Rust Red, Dark Gray
36. **Embarrassment** – Bright Red, Blush Pink, Soft Purple
37. **Frustration** – Burnt Orange, Deep Red, Charcoal Gray
38. **Annoyance** – Mustard Yellow, Reddish Orange, Muted Brown
39. **Anger** – Fiery Red, Black, Deep Crimson
40. **Resentment** – Dark Green, Deep Red, Murky Brown
41. **Disgust** – Sickly Green, Brown, Muddy Yellow
42. **Contempt** – Olive Green, Dark Gray, Rust Orange
43. **Hatred** – Black, Deep Crimson, Dark Purple
44. **Envy** – Dark Green, Acid Yellow, Emerald
45. **Jealousy** – Bright Green, Deep Blue, Reddish Purple
46. **Anxiety** – Pale Blue, Gray, Muted Violet
47. **Fear** – Dark Purple, Deep Blue, Shadow Gray
48. **Dread** – Black, Deep Blue, Murky Green
49. **Worry** – Soft Gray, Pale Yellow, Faded Blue
50. **Nervousness** – Light Gray, Soft Pink, Pale Orange

Mixed and Complex Emotions

51. **Nostalgia (Happiness + Sadness)** – Sepia, Muted Gold, Soft Purple
52. **Bittersweetness (Joy + Sadness)** – Dusty Rose, Golden Yellow, Deep Blue
53. **Love with Longing (Affection + Sadness)** – Soft Red, Muted Purple, Light Blue
54. **Schadenfreude (Joy + Maliciousness)** – Deep Purple, Acid Green, Crimson
55. **Guilty Pleasure (Enjoyment + Guilt)** – Dark Red, Soft Gold, Deep Purple
56. **Surprise (Neutral, but often mixed with Fear or Joy)** – Bright Yellow, Electric Blue, Soft White
57. **Relief (Joy + Previous Fear)** – Pale Green, Cool Blue, Soft Gray
58. **Gratification (Joy + Satisfaction)** – Golden Yellow, Warm Brown, Soft Pink
59. **Awe (Wonder + Admiration + Fear)** – Deep Indigo, Silver, Midnight Blue
60. **Betrayal (Anger + Sadness)** – Deep Red, Dark Gray, Murky Purple
61. **Insecurity (Fear + Self-Doubt)** – Pale Violet, Soft Gray, Faded Blue
62. **Hopefulness (Optimism + Uncertainty)** – Light Yellow, Soft Green, Muted Blue
63. **Alienation (Sadness + Disconnection)** – Dark Purple, Gray, Deep Blue
64. **Vindication (Relief + Resentment)** – Deep Red, Bronze, Muted Gold
65. **Anticipation (Excitement + Uncertainty)** – Bright Orange, Electric Blue, Pale Yellow

Mild and Low-Intensity Emotions

66. **Calmness** – Soft Blue, Pale Green, Gentle Gray
67. **Relaxation** – Warm Beige, Light Blue, Pastel Green
68. **Mild Amusement** – Light Purple, Soft Yellow, Pale Pink
69. **Light Curiosity** – Teal, Bright Green, Warm Yellow

70. **Slight Disappointment** – Faded Blue, Soft Brown, Muted Gray
71. **Mild Irritation** – Dusty Orange, Soft Red, Muted Brown
72. **Subtle Concern** – Pale Yellow, Light Gray, Muted Green
73. **Gentle Affection** – Soft Pink, Lavender, Light Coral
74. **Soft Admiration** – Warm Gold, Muted Violet, Light Blue
75. **Quiet Determination** – Deep Blue, Warm Brown, Soft Gray

Intense and Extreme Emotions

76. **Ecstasy (Intense Joy)** – Neon Pink, Golden Yellow, Fiery Orange
77. **Rage (Intense Anger)** – Blood Red, Black, Deep Purple
78. **Terror (Intense Fear)** – Pitch Black, Deep Indigo, Shadowy Gray
79. **Deep Despair (Intense Sadness)** – Dark Purple, Murky Blue, Heavy Gray
80. **Overwhelming Gratitude** – Bright Gold, Soft Green, Warm Peach
81. **Exhilaration (Intense Excitement)** – Neon Orange, Electric Blue, Hot Pink
82. **Deep Humiliation** – Crimson Red, Muted Purple, Dark Brown
83. **Intense Longing** – Deep Blue, Soft Rose, Muted Violet
84. **Overpowering Awe** – Cosmic Purple, Shimmering Silver, Midnight Blue
85. **Utter Hopelessness** – Black, Deep Gray, Murky Blue

Social and Moral Emotions

86. **Righteous Indignation (Anger + Moral Belief)** – Deep Crimson, Dark Gold, Fiery Orange
87. **Social Embarrassment (Shame in Public)** – Blush Pink, Soft Red, Pale Yellow
88. **Moral Disgust (Disapproval + Disgust)** – Murky Green, Deep Brown, Muted Yellow
89. **Compassionate Sorrow (Sadness for Others)** – Soft Blue, Gentle Gray, Warm Beige
90. **Protective Instinct (Love + Fear for Another's Safety)** – Deep Red, Midnight Blue, Warm Gold

Feel free to experiment with colors you are drawn to in nature or in an art store. Use your feelings to guide you in the process. Experiment with wearing clothing that brings more colors to your life. Take a risk and begin showing up in more colorful ways at home, work, and play. Color can not only create a healthier emotional life, but it can bring a new and refreshing energy to the world around you. Get out of your head and into your heart, and start having more fun with color.

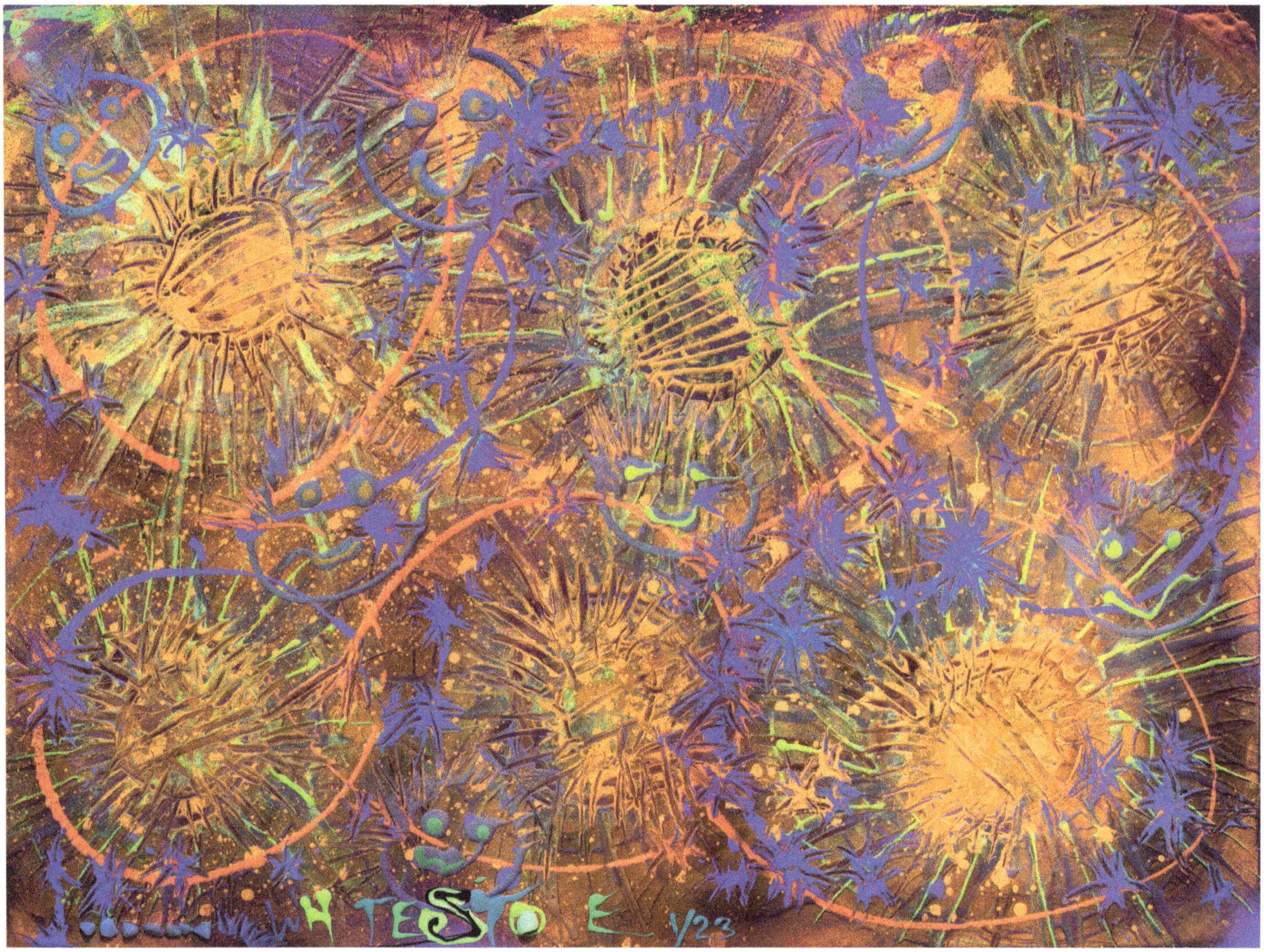

Heart Sutra

Learn the Heart Sutra. It will empower your life and you will meet yourself in the truest way.

Heart Sutra

The Heart Sutra is a sacred Buddhist text about emptiness and compassion. Here's my glow painting of the prayer: Scan the QR code to see the prayer on canvas come alive.

"Form is emptiness, emptiness is form. Form is not separate from emptiness, emptiness is not separate from form. What is form is emptiness, what is emptiness is form. The same is true of feelings, perceptions, mental formations, and consciousness. All things are empty; they are neither created nor destroyed, neither pure nor impure, neither increasing nor decreasing. Therefore, in emptiness there is no form, no feeling, no perception, no mental formation, no consciousness. No eye, ear, nose, tongue, body, or mind. No sight, sound, smell, taste, touch, or objects of mind. No realm of sight up to no realm of mind consciousness. No ignorance and no end to ignorance, up to no aging and death and no end to aging and death. No suffering, cause of suffering, cessation of suffering, or path. No wisdom and no attainment. Because there is nothing to attain, bodhisattvas rely on Prajnaparamita and their minds are without fear. Free from delusion, they attain nirvana. All buddhas of the past, present, and future rely on Prajnaparamita and attain unsurpassed, complete, perfect enlightenment. Therefore, know that Prajnaparamita is the great mantra, the mantra of great wisdom, the unsurpassed mantra, the unequalled mantra, which completely removes all suffering. This is truth, not falsehood.

Therefore, proclaim the Prajnaparamita mantra, proclaim the mantra which says: 'Gate, gate, paragate, parasamgate, bodhi svaha.'"

(Gone, gone, gone beyond, gone completely beyond, awakened, so be it.)

Sacred Between

Between intention and surrender, I discovered the sacred space where beauty births itself unbidden. Planning my mural carefully with sketches, I knew exactly what I wanted to create. But halfway through, spilled water blurred my careful lines. Frustrated tears welled up—until I saw how the "accident" created soft edges more beautiful than my rigid plan. My best art emerged in that magical middle place. I showed up with clear intention, then surrendered control to something beyond myself. Nature works this way too. DNA provides the blueprint, but environmental factors influence how each tree or animal develops. Many spiritual traditions honor this middle space between effort and letting go—prayer requires both speaking and listening.

New Year's Day

Every day is a new day? Can you find joy in your innocence today?

New Year's Day

When I painted these trees reaching toward that blazing sunrise, I was having one of those mornings when my heart felt super heavy. You know those days? When you wake up and your problems from yesterday are still there waiting?

I grabbed my brightest oranges and yellows because I needed to remind myself that the sun doesn't care what happened yesterday. It just shows up, every single morning, brand new, just like we can choose to be. Scan the QR code to see it shine.

Those tall trees? They're stretching up from the dark soil, through all the messy middle parts of life, reaching for the light. That's exactly how I feel sometimes—rooted in the complicated stuff but still growing toward something brighter.

The textured bark I created by building up layers and scraping them back shows all the rough patches we go through. But notice how the trees still stand tall? That's the cool thing about hard times—they don't have to break us.

When I look at this painting now, I remember that feeling of not knowing what's coming next, but trusting it anyway. The sun rises whether we understand why or not. New things are being born in us every day.

I painted this to remind myself (and now you) that everything really is unfolding *for* us, not against us—even when it's hard to see. The light always returns. Always. And all we need to do is keep reaching for it. What's the sunrise you're reaching for today?

Tangled Wisdom

The tangled roots beneath my feet taught me how strength grows in hidden directions. I used to think trees grew straight up, roots grew straight down. But when the old oak fell after storms, its exposed roots showed a wild, twisted system spreading in surprising ways. Some roots reached toward water sources. Others wrapped around rocks for stability. They didn't follow simple rules but responded to what they encountered underground. My own strength is like this—growing in directions nobody sees, sometimes wrapping around obstacles rather than fighting them. The strongest trees don't have perfect root systems; they have adaptable ones. Now when I face problems, I think of those tangled roots finding creative paths through hard soil. My heart's hidden roots reach where they need to, finding water and support in unexpected places, creating stability that others might not understand but that holds me secure through life's storms.

Flock of Glow

When everything falls apart, where is your soul?

Flock of Glow

When I painted this, I couldn't decide if I wanted to make birds or just splash colors everywhere. So I thought, "Why not both?"

I found at least seven birds hiding in this explosion of color! Can you spot them? The electric greens and hot pinks weren't colors I'd normally put together, but that day I felt like breaking rules. I wanted to make something that buzzed with energy, like when you can't sit still because you're so excited. You know that feeling?

I layered paint on paint, letting each color peek through from underneath. Sometimes I scraped back areas to reveal hidden colors, like uncovering buried treasure. The birds emerged from this chaos—some obvious, others hinted at with a wing shape or an eye.

I called it "Flow of Glow" because that's exactly how it felt while painting it—like glowing energy was flowing through my brush and onto the wood. The birds aren't realistic because they're not really birds—they're feelings taking flight. Scan the QR code to see how feelings change overnight.

When I look at this painting now, it reminds me that sometimes the most beautiful things happen when we stop trying to control everything and just let the colors dance. How many birds can you find? And what colors make you feel most alive?

Wilderness Between

Between heartbreak and healing lies a wilderness where wildflowers break through stone. When my best friend betrayed my trust, I felt like someone had dropped a heavy rock on my heart. The pain seemed permanent as concrete. But hiking through an abandoned lot, I noticed purple flowers growing up through cracked pavement. Nature showed me that broken places aren't the end of the story—they're often where new beauty begins. The space between being hurt and feeling better isn't empty wasteland; it's wild territory where unexpected growth happens. Those purple flowers didn't need perfect soil—they just needed the tiniest crack to reach toward sunlight. My heart's cracks similarly became perfect growing spots for courage and forgiveness, qualities that couldn't have sprouted in unbroken ground. Now I honor the wilderness between wound and healing as sacred space where life's most persistent gifts take root.

Australia

The most difficult journey in life is moving from your head to your heart. What price will you pay if you avoid the journey?

Australia

When I first stepped foot in Australia, I felt like my heart grew three sizes! Every sunrise, every beach, every weird and wild creature seemed to speak a secret language I somehow understood. This painting came straight from that feeling.

The sky is my favorite part. I layered pinks and golds and whites, blending them until they felt like those magical Australian sunsets that make you stop whatever you're doing just to stare. Remember seeing something so beautiful you got goosebumps? That's what those colors are trying to say. Scan the QR code to see the land fade into the light of the darkness.

Those black circles floating in the sky are the spirits of the land, visible only to those who hold the ancient ancestors who roam the sacred vast lands.

The coolest thing happened when I tried this under black light—suddenly all these hidden colors jumped out! I didn't paint what Australia looks like. I painted what Australia feels like when it gets inside your heart and touches your soul.

Have you ever been somewhere that felt like it was painting itself inside you?

Wound Watersheds

My wounds became watersheds, directing the flow of a life I couldn't imagine before. After heavy rain, I noticed how water always finds a path downhill, flowing around obstacles or creating new channels when blocked. The painful splits in my life—moving away from old friends, parents divorcing, dreams not attained—I used to see as damage. But like rain hitting hillsides, those hurts became watersheds that channeled my life in new directions I never would have chosen but led to unexpected good. Scientists say even small changes in a mountain ridge can completely change where water flows or which valleys get nourished. My heart's broken ridges similarly directed my life's rivers toward new territories I wouldn't have explored otherwise. Now I look at painful events with curious eyes, wondering, "What is this watershed creating? Where will this river of tears eventually lead me?" The answer is usually somewhere I couldn't have planned but needed to discover.

Mount Lily Lemmon No. 1

How flexible are you with change?

Mount Lily Lemmon No. 1

When I painted these trees reaching for the sky, I was trying to capture that feeling when something beautiful just stops you in your tracks. You know what I mean? Like when you're hiking along, thinking about regular stuff, and suddenly—BAM!—you see colors so vivid they make you forget everything else.

My daughter Lily took some amazing photos on Mount Lemmon in Tucson. The trees were showing off their fall colors, each branch a different shade of yellow, green, and coral pink. It looked like nature was painting the mountainside with liquid sunshine. Look closely to see a hundred glow stones speckled across the forest floor.

I chose that deep blue background because that's how the Arizona sky feels against autumn trees. There are two paintings in this series that blow up when the lights change. Scan the QR code to see my glow painting reach a new level. That's the magic of creating—sometimes your hands discover things your brain didn't even plan!

What autumn colors make your heart feel the most alive? Have you ever seen something in nature that was so beautiful it made you glow inside?

Sacred Text

I learned to read the sacred text written in bark and lichen, thunder and rain. Books taught me letters, but trees showed me a more ancient alphabet. Touching rough oak bark, I felt braille-like patterns telling stories of drought years and abundant seasons. Lightning-split trunks revealed paragraphs about survival and transformation. The green script of lichen growing on rocks taught lessons about partnership and patience. Nature writes in living ink that changes with seasons and weather—a holy book that's never complete. Indigenous elders speak of reading clouds and animal tracks the way others read scripture. I began noticing how birds arrange themselves on wires like musical notes, how falling leaves punctuate autumn with commas and exclamation points. This world-text doesn't need translation—it speaks directly to something older than my thinking mind. Now I walk through forests not as a visitor but as a student, learning to read the ongoing story written in everything around me.

Mount Lily Lemmon No. 2

What seeds are you planting in your sacred garden that can bloom and become your survival for the future?

Mount Lily Lemmon No.2

When I created this second painting in my Mount Lily Lemmon series, it felt like continuing a conversation with the trees themselves. There was so much color to explore. The bright yellows on the left show how the sunlight hit those trees first thing in the morning. The soft pinks on the right are the same trees, catching the last light of day. I wanted to show how the same trees can look totally different depending on when you see them.

As I painted the series of two glow paintings, I was humbled in advance that no matter how hard I tried, I could not create the same beauty that mother nature creates. I wanted to trust my vision and creativity. I spent hours applying and painting with the little drops of tile acrylic cement. I wanted the color of the leaves to rise off the canvas. I speckled hundreds of glow stones across the forest floor, just for fun, and it worked in creating something completely original. Scan the QR code to see the magic of black light and glow take effect.

This is number two in the series because one painting couldn't hold all the feelings that the photos of Mount Lemmon gave me. Sometimes the biggest feelings need more than one canvas, more than one try to get them just right.

What places have made you feel so much that you needed more than one way to remember them?

Language of Soil

The language of soil and seed revealed itself as I unlearned the dictionary of doing. Always busy with homework and chores, I thought value came from checking boxes. But gardening taught me different words. Seeds don't strive or schedule—they wait in darkness until conditions are right, then unfurl according to inner timing. Watching corn kernels swell and crack open underground made me question my rushing. Nature speaks a slower language of patience and becoming. The tomato doesn't force its ripening; the oak doesn't hurry toward its full height. Earthworms transform the ground not through ambition but through faithful presence. I began listening for this quiet vocabulary of being rather than doing—words like "unfold," "nurture," "receive," and "allow." My worth, I discovered, wasn't in my crowded calendar but in how I permitted life to root and blossom through me, following rhythms more ancient than clocks.

Ukraine Glows Forever

Do you believe non-violence is possible? What can you offer to bring more peace into the world? We need it more than ever

Ukraine Glows Forever

These dandelions are a symbol of hope against an ominous sun setting in the distant future. I was thinking about how dandelions grow anywhere, even in the harshest places, and how their seeds fly away to start new life somewhere else.

I titled it "Ukraine Glows Forever" because I truly believe that light can't be permanently dimmed. Not by war, not by hatred, not by anything. What glows from inside will always find a way to shine. I painted this work from a beautiful photograph that was posted online. The photograph is of an original painting by an unknown Ukrainian artist, and I was moved to paint a glow version of it.

I chose those fiery oranges and pinks for the sky because that's how hope feels to me—warm and bright, even when it's surrounded by darkness. You know how the sunset can make even an ordinary day feel special? That's what I wanted for Ukraine—a reminder that beauty still exists, even in painful times. The black stems might look delicate, but they're actually super strong. That's exactly like the people I was painting for—they might look breakable from far away, but up close, you can see their incredible strength. I made the dandelion seeds white and glowing because seeds carry futures inside them. Each one is a tiny wish, a small dream, waiting to be carried somewhere safe to grow. No matter how hard the wind blows, some seeds will always find good soil.

What are the dandelions in your life—the hopes that keep growing no matter what?

Wound Doorways

My wounds became doorways through which new light entered unbidden. That jagged crack in my heart where my marriage broke—I tried to patch over with brave smiles. But sitting by the river, watching how sunshine poured through broken storm clouds, I saw how nature uses breaks as passages for brilliance. Like the lightning-split oak now housing golden honey bees in its scorched hollow, my painful splits became sacred entrances. Through them poured unexpected warmth: compassion I never knew I could feel, strength hidden beneath my fear. The places that hurt most became the very spots where stars sneaked into my darkness. Now I touch my scars gently, with gratitude, recognizing each as a doorway carved by life's rough hands through which new light arrives without asking permission.

Free Will

Have you embraced the gift of free will? Have you integrated the boxes that keep you from living a shame- and guilt-free life?

Free Will

When I named this painting "Free Will," I wasn't just talking about my client, Will. I was talking about something we all are searching for—the chance to break out of the boxes we didn't even know we put ourselves in.

Will had been stuck in rehab for too long. But the real prison? It was the tiny boxes inside his mind, telling him who he was supposed to be. You probably know those boxes too—the ones that whisper, "You can't," or, "You shouldn't," or, "What will people think?"

Nature became Will's teacher. When you lie against a massive tree or look up at stars that have been shining for billions of years, your problems don't look so giant anymore. Your heart can finally take a deep breath and say, "Oh, I'm pretty small ... and that's awesome! These boxes are my own creation, and I can set myself free, because I've been given the gift of free will."

I painted this wild and messy, because healing is wild and messy. There's no straight path through the forest of our feelings. But when we honor them—really listen to what they're trying to tell us—they become our best compass for navigating change.

What boxes are holding you that might need some wildness to crack them open? Scan the QR code and see the boxes appear in the dark with *love* at the top to help set us free.

Lost Rivers

The canyon of loss carved rivers for grace to flow unbidden. When my best friend moved away, it felt like someone dug a huge hole in my heart. That empty space hurt so much! But then something weird happened—the hole started to fill with new feelings. I felt more kindness toward the new kid who seemed lost. I appreciated my other friends more. It's like when rain carves paths down a dirt hill—at first it looks ruined, but then those paths help new water flow exactly where it needs to go. My sadness made deep paths in me that allowed good things to flow into places they couldn't reach before. I didn't ask for this or make it happen—the good stuff just knew how to find those new rivers my loss had created.

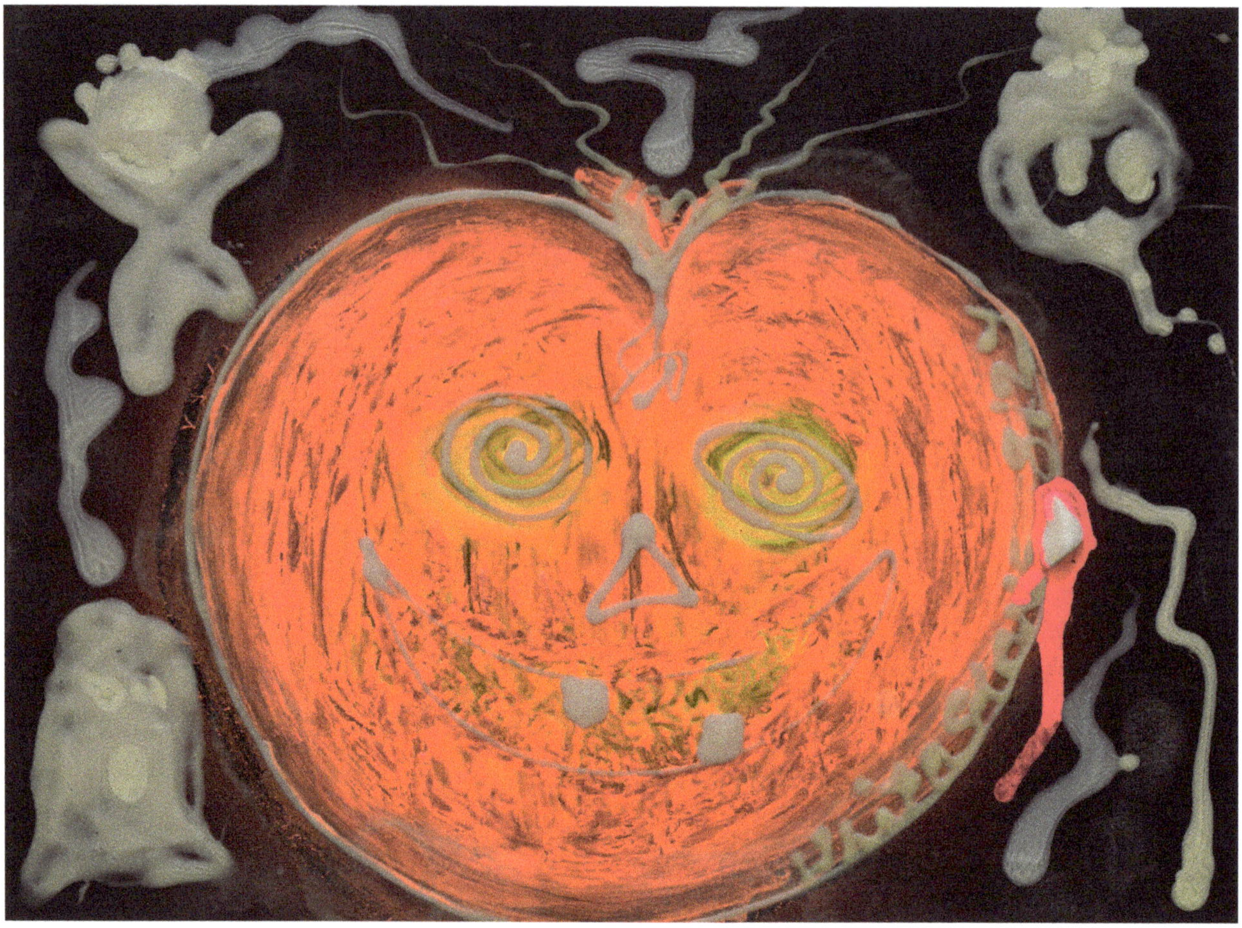

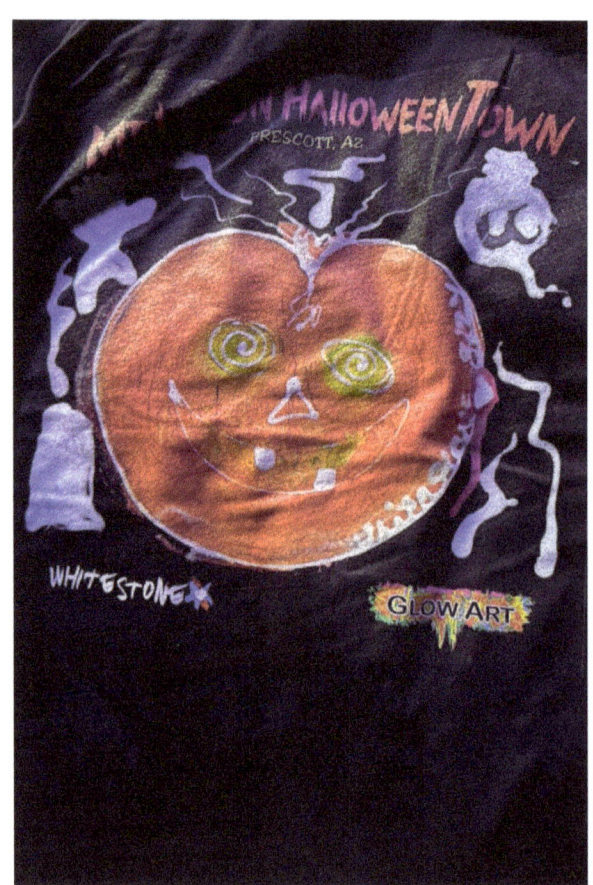

Haunted Pumpkin

What does it feel like to fall apart? Can you express that feeling with pen and paper or paint and canvas? Share it on social media or with a good friend.

Haunted Pumpkin

When I painted this glowing pumpkin, I was thinking about how we all have parts we keep hidden. You know those thoughts or feelings that seem too weird or scary to show other people? I was thrilled when the "Haunted Pumpkin" became my first commercial success. All three versions have been printed on special Halloween Town t-shirts available on my website. Scan the QR code to see the pumpkin come alive.

During Halloween, something magical happens. Suddenly, it's okay to let our spooky side out to play! We can wear costumes, make scary faces, and nobody thinks twice about it. For one night, we get to show parts of ourselves that usually stay in the shadows. I made this pumpkin's eyes into swirls because sometimes our deepest feelings don't look like regular emotions—they twist and turn and don't make perfect sense. That's totally normal, even if it feels strange.

The glowing blue and green paint was my favorite part to add. Under regular light, this painting looks pretty ordinary. But when the lights go out—BAM!—all the hidden stuff becomes the star of the show. I love that moment when people first see it glow and their faces light up with surprise.

Sometimes I wonder if our "hidden" parts are actually our most interesting parts. Maybe the stuff we think is too strange to share is exactly what makes us special.

What parts of yourself do you only let out on Halloween?

Unraveling Text

My unraveling became a sacred text written in fallen leaves. When I lost my way and felt like I was coming apart—like an old sweater with threads pulling loose—I thought I was ruined. But walking through the forest that autumn, I watched leaves falling. Each one drifted down in its own special way, making patterns on the ground. I realized my coming-apart wasn't random or bad—it was making a beautiful pattern too. The parts of me that were changing and falling away were spelling out an important message, like the leaves that wrote stories on the forest floor. Other people could learn from watching my journey, just like I learned from watching nature. My hardest moments weren't just mess and confusion—they were creating something meaningful, a special story that only I could tell.

Let Something Wild Loose

Can you allow yourself to feel everything? Can you take a private walk in nature, remove your clothing, and let your wild one loose? How can you express that experience in a healthy way?

Let Something Wild Loose

When I painted this face, I didn't plan it—I just let my hands do whatever they wanted. It felt like setting a wild animal free after keeping it in a cage too long. Have you ever felt that way? Like there's something inside you jumping to get out?

Those swirling yellow eyes weren't supposed to be eyes at first. They are also a woman's breasts. The breasts turned into eyes staring back at me from the canvas, almost like they were saying, "Finally! You're letting us out!" I wrote, "LET SOMETHING WILD LOOSE," across the top because that's exactly what was happening. The brown strands that look like hair? I painted them as arms. You can use your imagination by looking closely at the tiny beads that spell out "Pleasure Zone" because that's what making this felt like—pure pleasure without worrying if it was "good" or not. I forgot about the rules and let my imagination run wild.

When I look at this now, I see parts of myself I usually keep hidden—the weird thoughts, the big feelings that don't always make sense. What wild thing inside you is waiting to come out and play? What would happen if you let it loose, even for a little while? Scan the QR code to see it glow.

Empty Cradle

The canvas taught me that emptiness holds all possibilities, just as the dark earth cradles dormant seeds. Winter fields look dead and empty, but farmers know better—beneath that bare surface, seeds wait patiently for spring's signal to grow. My empty canvas scared me at first. What if I had no good ideas? What if I ruined it? But sitting with that clean white space, I began feeling its special power. Empty doesn't mean nothing; it means everything-not-yet-decided. Many wisdom traditions honor emptiness—the Japanese concept of *ma* celebrates empty space in art as where possibility lives. Bird nests and cupped hands show how emptiness creates useful holding places. When I stopped seeing the blank canvas as something to quickly fill with "good" art and started respecting its emptiness as sacred waiting space, my creativity changed completely. Now, before starting a new project, I honor the empty moment, the unplanted field, the open hands—knowing these apparent voids actually cradle all possible futures, just waiting for the right moment to sprout.

Shadow Glow Guardian

The shadows aren't the enemy. They're just waiting for an invitation to dance.

Shadow Glow Guardian

When I painted this shadow-fly, I was trying to capture a magical moment that happened to me in Brazil. Have you ever caught a glimpse of yourself in a mirror or window and for a split second, didn't recognize who you were looking at? That's what happened to me. I was walking at night near the jungle outside Rio when my shadow fell across a wall that had a butterfly painting. In that weird, wonderful moment, my shadow wasn't just a dark outline of me anymore—it became something with wings! Something that could fly! The raised squiggly lines feel like jungle vines to me, wrapping around but never trapping.

When I look at this painting now, it reminds me that we're all more than we think we are. Sometimes we need to see our shadow in a different place to realize we've had wings all along. Scan the QR code to see it glow in the dark.

What parts of yourself are waiting to transform? What wings might you discover if you looked at your shadow from a different angle?

Dancing With Our Shadows

Have you ever noticed how your shadow stretches and bends when you move near a light? It's always there, but we don't always pay attention to it. That's kind of how our inner shadows work too—those parts of ourselves that we try to hide or ignore.

Shadow dancing happens when we finally turn around and say hello to these darker parts. It feels scary at first, like walking into a dark room. But once you turn on the light, you realize there's treasure hidden there.

When I let myself shadow dance, I discover that my jealousy can teach me what I truly value. My anger shows me what matters most. My fear points to what I love. These feelings aren't monsters—they're messengers carrying important news from deep inside.

The cool thing about shadow dancing is that it gives us more energy. Hiding parts of ourselves takes a lot of work! When we stop pushing those parts away, we suddenly have all this extra power to create, to connect, to be fully alive.

Our shadows also connect us to each other. When I admit I sometimes feel small or scared or not good enough, it creates a bridge where other people can walk over and say, "Me too." And isn't that what we all want? To be seen completely and still be loved?

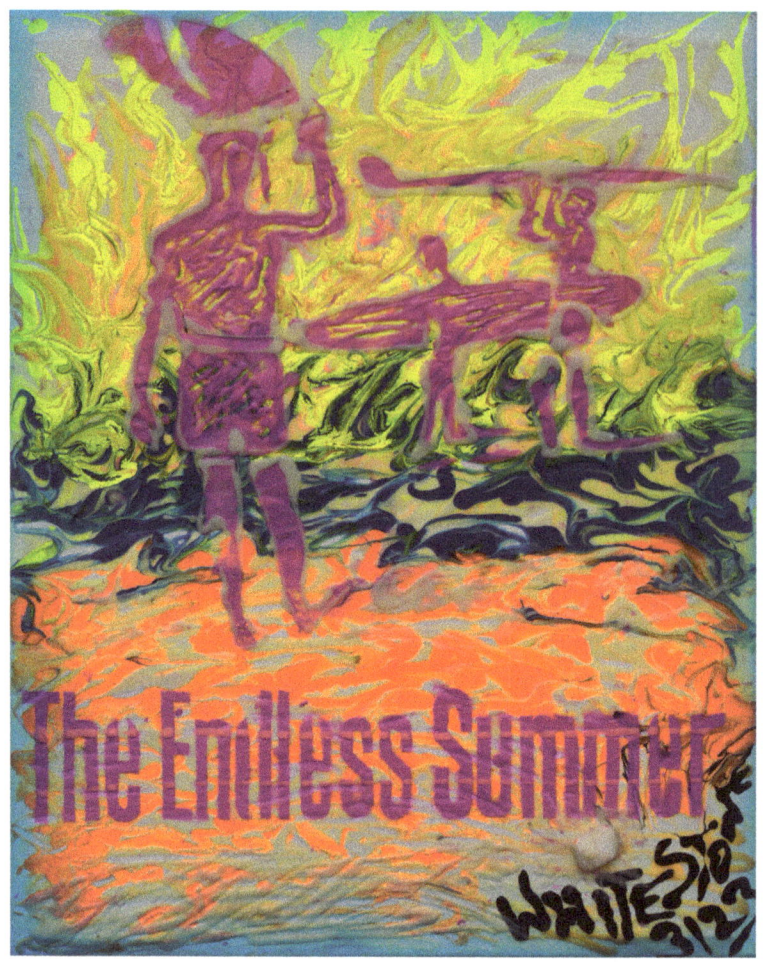

The Endless Summer

How does the ocean open up your imagination?

The Endless Summer

"The Endless Summer" series was my first commissioned project for the inaugural Dana Point Film Festival in California. I created five glow paintings under license with "The Endless Summer" logo, the iconic brand based on what is considered the most-watched surf documentary of all time.

I noticed how the surfers' bodies told stories their words couldn't yet explain—stories about courage, joy, and perfect freedom. These men without faces represent the millions who have found the beach and surf to be a playground for the soul.

Make sure to scan the QR code to see how the landscape changes and enjoy my attempt at bringing the iconic logo and film back to life in a new way. My own experience of surfing was fuel for creating these glow paintings. After a good session, there's an internal satisfaction and glow that comes from a day spent with the surf and sun.

Note: The first four paintings in the "Endless Summer Series" sold at auction at the film festival. These works are considered classic, one-of-a-kind collector's items for people who love the film and the worldwide lifestyle it birthed.

Ocean's Whisper

Have you ever noticed how the ocean seems to know exactly what you're feeling? Whether you're happy, confused, or carrying something heavy inside, the waves somehow match your mood perfectly.

The ocean does this amazing thing when you spend time with it—it helps your emotions move instead of getting stuck. In … out. The waves, like breath, rise and fall. It's like the ocean teaches your body how to let feelings flow through you instead of getting jammed up inside.

Those times when your head feels too full of thoughts? The ocean's vastness gives all that mental noise somewhere to spread out. Your problems don't seem so huge anymore when you're looking at something that stretches beyond what your eyes can see.

The salt water, the changing tides, the way light dances on the surface—these things speak to parts of us that don't use words. They wake up the creative voice that lives in your feelings, not your thoughts. The water reminds us that creativity isn't something we control—it's something we allow, just like the tide coming in and going out again.

PART NINE

Sharing Our Glow: A Journey into Emotional Wilderness

"In wilderness, we discover our luminous stone buried beneath the sediment of distraction; in feeling everything—storms and sunshine alike—we begin the patient polishing; and through creating without reservation or apology, our essential light finally finds its way home, casting its particular glow across a world hungry for authentic fire." —Mary Oliver

The Invitation of Wild Spaces

In the cathedral of ancient redwoods, where light filters through branches in golden shafts, there exists a silence that speaks volumes. This eloquent hush carries an invitation—to shed the protective layers we've wrapped around our hearts, to dissolve the boundaries between inner and outer landscapes, to remember our place in the grand symphony of living things. Nature extends this wordless welcome not as luxury but as birthright, a return to the primordial conversation our ancestors knew intimately.

"Art washes away from the soul the dust of everyday life," Picasso reminded us. But before art can perform this sacred ablution, we must first gather the waters—the raw emotions, the unfiltered experiences, the direct perceptions that flow from full-bodied presence. These waters spring most abundantly in wild places, where the manufactured certainties of human systems give way to older, wiser rhythms.

What might emerge if you committed to this gathering? If you set aside time—not as an occasional indulgence but as an essential practice—to stand barefoot at the threshold between worlds? If you allowed the hundred emotions identified in the Geneva Emotion Wheel to rise and fall without resistance, each one a distinct hue in the spectrum of your becoming?

The Polishing of the Stone

Within each human heart lies a stone of peculiar luminosity—not placed there by random chance but grown through the precise pressures of your unique journey. This stone contains your particular radiance, the quality of light that only you can contribute to the world's illumination. Yet stones do not reveal their inner fire without friction. The very resistance that seems to obscure your brightness serves as the necessary abrasion that gradually, patiently reveals your glow.

"Breathing is the greatest pleasure in life. Art is the second greatest," observed Marty Rubin. These seemingly simple acts—drawing air into body, drawing feeling into form—create the essential rhythm for polishing your inner stone. Each conscious breath carried through challenging emotions serves as a gentle abrasive; each creative expression smooths another surface until reflection becomes possible.

The wilderness offers ideal conditions for this refinement. Against the vast backdrop of mountains, beneath the infinite canvas of sky, surrounded by the exuberant improvisation of living systems, your stone's true nature emerges with greater clarity. Here, emotions can be experienced at their full magnitude without the diminishing effects of enclosed spaces and social constraints. Here, the friction between your current self and your becoming self finds perfectly calibrated resistance—strong enough to transform, gentle enough to preserve the stone's essential character.

The Hundred-Hued Emotional Landscape

Across the vast terrain of human experience, a hundred emotions bloom like wildflowers after rain—some brilliant and demanding our attention, others subtle and easily overlooked, many growing entangled at their roots. To navigate this wilderness of feeling is to embark on the most profound adventure of existence—learning that joy's summit appears more magnificent for having traversed sorrow's valley, that courage blossoms from fear's fertile soil, that peace emerges not from emotional absence but from embracing the complete spectrum with open arms.

Our emotional intelligence develops not through selectively cultivating pleasant states while weeding out difficult ones, but through creating hospitable conditions for all feelings to reveal their particular wisdom. Like a diverse ecosystem where each species serves essential functions, our full emotional spectrum creates resilience, adaptability, and generative potential unavailable to more restricted internal environments.

When we wander in natural settings, the "wild monkey mind" that chatters incessantly through indoor hours gradually quiets—not because thinking ceases, but because it shifts from fragmented anxiety to integrated awareness. The breathing patterns that constrict in artificial environments naturally deepen in response to fresh air, open space, and visual horizons that extend beyond walls. This physiological recalibration creates the internal conditions where emotions can be experienced as weather systems moving through vast awareness rather than confined storms threatening to overwhelm limited identity.

The Alchemy of Transformation

Once gathered, these emotional waters seek channels for expression. The creative impulse isn't separate from emotional intelligence but is its natural extension—the desire to give tangible form to internal experience. This alchemy transforms feeling into creation through infinite pathways.

Art becomes the visible manifestation of invisible currents, translating emotional texture into color, line, form, and composition. The canvas offers a container large enough to hold contradictory feelings simultaneously, revealing relationships between apparently opposing states that logical thought cannot reconcile. Through visual expression, emotions that seemed chaotic or overwhelming when contained within find coherence and meaning when externalized through creative vision.

Writing provides architecture for emotional exploration, creating structures that support deeper understanding without simplifying complexity. Whether through personal narrative that traces the meandering path of a single feeling, poetry that distills emotional essence into concentrated language, or fictional worlds that embody psychological landscapes, writing transforms amorphous experience into communicable form without diminishing its living mystery.

Music captures the temporal nature of emotional experience—how feelings arise, intensify, transform, and dissolve in continuous flow. Through melody, harmony, rhythm, and silence, music creates emotional narratives that honor both the pattern and unpredictability of our inner weather. The musician learns that every feeling state, from profound grief to ecstatic joy, offers unique tonal qualities essential to the complete composition.

Even the seemingly mundane domains of daily life become vessels for emotional intelligence when approached with creative awareness:

The food we prepare and share becomes a sensory expression of our inner state—whether through the nurturing comfort of slow-simmered stews during periods of vulnerability, the vibrant celebration of colorful feasts during joyful gathering, or the careful attention to subtle flavors during contemplative solitude. Cooking informed by emotional presence transforms mere sustenance into communion, each dish a poem composed of texture, aroma, flavor, and intention.

Our clothing choices, released from mere fashion conformity, become another language for emotional expression—the protective layers needed during sensitive periods, the expansive color choices during creative phases, the simplified forms during times requiring focus and clarity. The body wrapped in fabrics chosen with emotional intelligence becomes a moving sculpture, visual poetry expressing inner weather through external form.

The homes we create reflect not just aesthetic preference but emotional intelligence—spaces designed to support the full spectrum of human feeling rather than merely projecting curated identity. Rooms that invite both solitary reflection and genuine connection, materials that engage multiple senses, arrangements that honor both beauty and function—these choices emerge from understanding our emotional needs beyond superficial wants.

Even relationships become creative acts when informed by emotional awareness. Each interaction offers an opportunity to translate inner experience into shared understanding through the mediums of language, gesture, presence, and responsive listening. The emotionally intelligent relationship becomes a collaborative art form—a continuous improvisation requiring both vulnerability and skill, receptivity and expression.

The Compass of Compassion

As we develop fluency in our emotional language through nature immersion and creative expression, something remarkable emerges—genuine compassion for others navigating their internal wilderness. This isn't sentimental projection but clear recognition, born from intimate familiarity with the common territories of human experience.

Having traversed our valleys of grief, we recognize the particular posture of someone carrying similar weight. Having stood on our peaks of achievement, we understand both the exhilaration and unexpected emptiness that can accompany such heights. Having weathered storms of anger, fear, or confusion, we develop practical wisdom about navigating intensity without becoming submerged.

This compassion becomes not just an orientation toward others but a reliable internal compass. When emotions are no longer experienced as threats or interruptions but as essential information about our relationship with life, they guide rather than derail our journey. The same intensity that once seemed overwhelming becomes a trustworthy navigation system when we learn to read its signals accurately.

Maya Angelou observed that "the truest and most moving landscapes of human emotion are mapped across our faces, sculpted through our actions, and painted on the canvas of our relationships." These living maps develop detail and accuracy through regular expeditions into our emotional terrain—not from a safe distance but through direct immersion, through the messy, glorious process of feeling everything without selective avoidance.

The Weather and the Sky

Life's storms arrive regardless of our preparation or preference. Financial uncertainty, relationship challenges, health concerns, societal upheaval—these weather systems move through personal and collective experience with natural force beyond individual control. What remains within our influence is not whether storms occur but how we meet them—whether we face changing conditions with rigid resistance or resilient response.

Nature demonstrates this wisdom continuously. The flexible willow bending in hurricane winds often survives while the rigid oak snaps. The forest adapting to changing climate conditions through diversity thrives while monocultures collapse. The river, finding new channels after the landslide, continues its journey while water fighting gravity remains stagnant.

When we commit to regular immersion in natural settings, while embracing our full emotional spectrum, we develop this same adaptive resilience. We learn to distinguish between the changing weather of circumstance and the unchanging sky of awareness that holds all conditions without being defined by any particular storm or clear day.

This doesn't mean achieving some permanent state of detached serenity. It means developing the internal spaciousness to experience life's complete range—from crushing disappointment to transcendent joy, from smoldering anger to expansive peace—without any single state becoming our entire identity. Like the sky that remains vast regardless of whether clouds, storms, or clear blue dominate any given day, our essential nature remains undiminished by emotional weather moving through it.

Finding and Sharing Our Glow

The stone within your heart—that particular quality of radiance unique to your journey—doesn't illuminate through effort or achievement. It glows when the layers obscuring it have been gently, persistently worn away through honest presence with everything life brings. This isn't a spiritual metaphor but practical reality: the development of emotional intelligence through nature connection and creative expression gradually reveals capacities for presence, resilience, and authentic engagement previously hidden beneath adaptive patterns.

Finding your glow means discovering that the very aspects of yourself you've been taught to hide, fix, or transcend often contain your most essential gifts. The sensitivity that seemed like weakness becomes your capacity for nuanced perception. The intensity that appeared overwhelming transforms into passionate engagement. The peculiar angles of your personality that didn't fit conventional molds reveal themselves as unique perspectives essential to the larger human conversation.

Sharing this glow doesn't require grand gestures or public platforms. It happens naturally through the quality of presence you bring to ordinary interactions, through the authentic expression that emerges when internal censorship dissolves, through the compassionate witnessing you offer others navigating similar terrain. Like bioluminescent organisms in ocean depths, your natural radiance serves not just personal expression but collective illumination—helping others locate their own light in shadowed times.

So I say now as Whitestone, The Glow Artist, "Dive into your art like a child plunging into ocean waves—with abandon, delight, and the thrilling certainty that even if you tumble, you'll rise again laughing, salt-kissed and transformed." This invitation extends beyond formal artistic practice to the creative act of living itself—the continuous improvisation required to navigate changing internal and external landscapes with both structure and spontaneity, discipline and surrender.

The Practice of Presence

Begin with a commitment to regular nature immersion—not as an occasional escape but as an essential practice in emotional intelligence. Set aside specific times for wilderness wandering without devices, distractions, or destinations. Whether in vast national parks or urban green spaces, these excursions create necessary conditions for emotional recalibration and creative renewal.

Develop rituals for transitioning between environments. Before entering natural settings, acknowledge your intention to receive whatever arises without selective filtering. Upon returning to constructed environments, create an intentional bridge to carry expanded awareness back into daily life rather than immediately reabsorbing limited perspectives.

Practice conscious breathing as a foundation for emotional presence. Notice how respiratory patterns reflect and reinforce emotional states—the shallow breath of anxiety, the held breath of anticipation, the deep sighs of release. Experiment with deliberately changing breath to create internal spaciousness for challenging emotions rather than attempting to transform feelings directly.

Establish regular creative practice as a channel for emotional expression. Whether through visual art, writing, music, movement, cooking, or other forms, develop the discipline of showing up consistently without attachment to particular outcomes. Create a container for emotional energy to find appropriate form without censorship or premature shaping.

Cultivate a community that honors emotional intelligence as essential wisdom rather than an inconvenient disruption. Surround yourself with others committed to authentic presence rather than perpetual positivity, with fellow explorers willing to acknowledge both shadow and light in human experience.

Remember that life happens for us, not to us. This perspective emerges not from intellectual reframing but from directly experiencing how apparently difficult circumstances often catalyze essential growth, how resistance typically creates suffering while acceptance opens pathways for creative response. The wilderness teaches this wisdom through every storm that nourishes soil, every fallen tree that creates habitat for new life, every challenging terrain that develops necessary strength.

The Continuous Unfolding

Finding and sharing your glow isn't a destination but is continuous unfolding—the gradual revelation of capacities always present but previously obscured. The stone doesn't become luminous; it already contains this quality. The polishing process merely removes what prevents its natural radiance from being visible.

Similarly, your emotional intelligence, creative essence, and authentic presence aren't qualities to achieve but are natural capacities to uncover through committed practice. Each venture into wild landscapes, each honest encounter with your complete emotional spectrum, each creative expression born from this engagement—serves as a gentle abrasion removing accumulated layers of protection, performance, and partial identity.

What emerges through this process isn't some perfected self but your original nature—the quality of presence that existed before adaptive patterns formed, the way of seeing untainted by others' expectations, the voice that speaks your particular truth without apology or exaggeration. This revealing requires courage and gentleness, discipline and patience, structured practice and surrendered trust.

The invitation stands: to gather emotional waters from wilderness immersion, to transform these waters into creative expression, to polish your inner stone through continuous presence with life's complete spectrum, to share your particular glow through authentic engagement with the world. Not because doing so leads to achievement or accolade, but because this practice returns you to the natural state of aligned participation with life's unfolding miracle.

As Vincent Van Gogh observed, "When I draw, I breathe differently. When I paint, my breath follows the rhythms of the colors." This simple statement holds profound wisdom about the relationship between creative expression and embodied presence. When we engage authentically with both inner and outer landscapes, our very physiology changes—breaths deepen, perception clarifies, defensive postures soften, creative channels open.

The hundred emotions identified in the Geneva Emotion Wheel—from the most challenging to the most uplifting—serve essential functions in this continuous unfolding. None need be rejected, none artificially cultivated. All belong in the complete ecosystem of human experience, each contributing particular nutrients to the soil from which your authentic expression grows.

In the end, sharing your glow becomes not something you achieve but something you allow—the natural illumination that occurs when artificial barriers between inner and outer landscapes dissolve through committed practice. The stone reveals its luminosity not through force but through patient, persistent engagement with the very elements that seem to obscure it. Your particular light emerges not despite life's challenges but because of your willingness to meet them with creative presence, moment by moment, breath by breath, step by wilderness step.

I have to state a universal truth over and over again. No matter how dark it gets, there is always more light. It's time to trust and get more curious about what's deep inside our inner world. I can assure you that the fears holding you back from that exploration are just the parts of the mind that are keeping you safe. Once you honor and celebrate their service, they will let loose of their crippling grip. Like children who were raised believing they had to protect their parents, they are dying for your love and affection. Once they know they have done their job, they will simply come along for the extraordinary life of creating something new and beautiful. Once you move forward, I assure you, they will continue reminding you that you need them to be safe, but with regular love and affection from your higher self, they will always go along for the ride.

We can explore this more together in the Whitestone Wanderlust section of this book.

The Weeping St. Francis

Have you had time to learn about St. Francis of Assisi? (If not, please do.)

The Weeping St. Francis

When I painted St. Francis with tears streaming down his face and a sunburst halo, I was trying to capture what made him revolutionary—his radical surrender to joy through deep grief and letting go—and look at what he became. I once read that St. Francis wept for most of his life—tears of grief and of joy. The tears showed up by mistake as the paint dripped while painting his eyes and ran down the wood's surface like tears. So I named the piece "The Weeping Francis." St. Francis walked the ultimate path of release. Born into wealth, he stripped naked in the town square, abandoning his inheritance and social position. This wasn't just symbolic drama. By emptying his hands of possessions, his heart could finally fill with wonder. After his conversion, he wore only rags and sandals. I honor all the paintings and pictures I've seen, but in my mind he was a king, so I dressed him in colors and clothes like a true king. This is oil on canvas with no glow effect. It speaks for itself. Many sizes can be had on the website.

What makes Francis the perfect patron saint for *The Art of Letting Go to Glow* is how his emptiness created fullness. As he shed layers of status and security, something luminous emerged. He didn't just talk about cosmic connection—he lived it by calling the sun his brother and the moon his sister. Birds rested on his shoulders because they sensed no grasping energy in him.

While theologians debated Christ's nature in lofty towers, Francis embodied Christ's message through simple actions—kissing lepers, negotiating peace with a wolf, rebuilding broken churches with his bare hands. He created a bridge between the divine cosmic Christ and the human Jesus by living as if they were one reality.

Lost Compass

In becoming lost, I shed the false compass of certainty. I used to think I had to know exactly where I was going all the time. I had this invisible compass in my head that pointed to "being right" instead of true north. But when I got lost in the meadow during fog, something amazing happened—I had to put down the need to be certain about everything. Without my know-it-all compass, I noticed so many things I usually missed: the different smells of wet grass, how spiderwebs caught drops of fog, the way birds called to each other through the mist. Being lost taught me that not knowing can be a gift. It's like taking off heavy shoes you didn't realize were hurting your feet. Now I don't panic when I don't have all the answers—I just look around with fresh eyes to see what the uncertainty might show me.

The Whitestone Dreamporium Glow Gallery

If you had the money, the time, and excitement to try something completely crazy but original, what would it be?

The Whitestone Dreamporium Glow Gallery: Can you ever lose at dreaming?

When I was a kid, my sister and I would sneak into our closets with pens and paint, creating wild art on hidden walls where our parents wouldn't find it. We built secret forts in the attic where our imaginations could run free. Something about those forbidden creative spaces stuck with me all these years—that feeling of making something totally yours in a world full of rules.

Years later, after watching a documentary about street art and learning from my art teacher Aviva that "paintings have souls" and "want to be seen," I decided to bring my childhood dream to life in the most spectacular way. I rented a 1,500-square-foot commercial space and transformed it into something magical: Whitestone Dreamporium.

I painted every wall black, installed regular lights and black lights with special switches, and created a space where art could literally glow in the dark. For six months, I built this dream using only materials that appeared in my life—thrift store finds, street donations, and things I already owned. It felt like the universe was helping me, sending exactly what I needed at exactly the right time.

Inside those black walls, I finally had permission to create without limits—that childhood joy of making wild, colorful art in a space that was completely mine. I made stickers, displayed my glowing artwork, and opened the doors to share this dream with others.

For eighteen months, college students and curious visitors came through with wide eyes and amazement. They loved it! But in Prescott, Arizona—mostly a retirement community—not enough people came to keep it financially alive. At $1,700 per month, the Dreamporium became an expensive experiment in following my creative fire.

It took six months to build and just half a day to close down. While it didn't make financial sense, I never regretted creating it. The Dreamporium taught me something important: our wildest dreams deserve space in the real world, even if only for a while. Sometimes the value isn't in making money but in making memories, in documenting the journey, and in proving to yourself that you dared to bring something truly original to life.

I still have the photos, videos, and memories of that glowing black-light gallery. Maybe someday they'll end up in a documentary, but for now, they remind me that creative fire doesn't always need to make sense—it just needs to burn bright enough to light up the darkness, even if only for a moment.

Leonard The Cosmic Lion

Shalom

Glow Paint

Whitestone's Glow Paint Adventure

I never planned to make paintings that glow in the dark. It happened by accident, like finding a secret door in your own house! When I first started painting, I just picked colors that made me feel happy, excited and alive. The bright fluorescent paints caught my eye at the art store, so I brought them home. I didn't know why I loved these colors so much—they just felt right to my invisible soul.

Then one night, something magical happened. My daughter turned off the lights while I was showing her my latest painting, and we both gasped. Parts of my artwork were glowing in the darkness! It was like my painting grew a secret life when no one was looking. I felt like I had discovered a hidden superpower in my art. After that night, I went on a treasure hunt, obsessed with finding more paints that would glow. These aren't your regular school art supplies—they're super special (and pretty expensive too). But the glow effect is worth every penny.

I learned to paint without any fancy art classes. My mentor was the extraordinary art teacher and author of *Painting From The Source*, Aviva Gold. She started me on big sheets of newsprint paper—the kind newspapers are printed on. I could tape sheets together to make giant canvases. My painting could grow as big as my imagination! I painted my first big artwork, "Leonardo the Space Lion," in a castle in Switzerland. Imagine being the only boy in art class—that was me, surrounded by 40 women who were all exploring their creativity! Iwas super nervous at first, but they became my biggest cheerleaders.

Leonardo is *huge*—like the size of your bedroom wall! The cool thing? He's actually hiding a secret. Underneath all that lion awesomeness is another painting called "Shalom" with big red veins reaching up toward space. That's my red handprint on the moon. Sometimes it's best to get your hands dirty. I didn't erase my first painting—I built on top of it! Aviva taught me something that changed how I make art forever: don't be afraid to paint over stuff. Just because you started with one idea doesn't mean you have to stick with it. Sometimes the best part of your art is letting it surprise you! Now whenever I paint, I remember both Leonardo and the hidden Shalom beneath him. That's what I think art is really about—making peace with the messy feelings inside and turning them into something beautiful. Just like how we grow and change as people!

Want to try glow painting yourself? Yes, they cost more than regular paints, but they'll make your artwork come alive in two different worlds—one with the lights on and another magical version when darkness falls. Add some UV paints and you'll be a glow artist. Your creativity doesn't have to stay flat on the page—it can dance between worlds, just like you can dance between feeling everything deeply and making something beautiful from those feelings. The expensive reality of these Glow Paints is why the Whitestone Art has become a collector's dream.

Whitestone's WanderLust Map

What are you doing with your one wild and crazy life?

Whitestone's WanderLust Map

When I painted this, I felt like I was drawing a treasure map to my own heart—. Nnot the kind of map that shows roads and cities, but one that shows all the most important parts of my psyche that I have learned to integrate into every aspect of my life.

I was so inspired by Bill Plotkin's Wild Mind Map.! Have you ever felt like there are different versions of you inside? Sometimes you're brave, sometimes creative, sometimes quiet? Plotkin taught me that these aren"t random— - they're actual parts of our souls that we're born with.

The swirling center with "WANDER ME LOST YOU FOUND LUST MAP" represents how sometimes we have to get totally lost to actually find ourselves. I painted that turquoise spiral in the middle because that's what my soul journey felt like— - spinning inward until I reached something true. When this painting glows under blacklight, it's like seeing the hidden magic that lives beneath everyday life.

The words scattered across the canvas— - "RADICAL SELF CARE," "BIG PICTURE," "TRUST MYSTERY," "GIVE BACK," "FEEL EVERYTHING"— - these are the guideposts I found during my wilderness quest. It's like each one lit up at different moments, showing me which way to walk next. During my many years of wandering, I received my spirit names: Whitestone, King(queendom) Dreamer, and Dragon Poet Slayer. What would your soul map look like? What words would guide you? What colors would show how it feels to be fully, completely you? Make sure youand scan the QR Ccode to see the map glow.

Time Spiral

Time revealed itself as a spiral rather than a line when viewed through wilderness eyes. I used to think of time like a straight ruler—Monday, Tuesday, Wednesday marching forward in a boring line. But watching seasons change in the forest showed me something different. Spring comes around again each year, but it's never exactly the same spring. The maple tree doesn't return to being a sapling; it grows taller with each spiral of seasons. Many indigenous people see time this way—as circular but always developing, like a spiral moving forward while turning. Looking at tree rings helped me understand—each circle marks another year, but also shows the tree getting wider. Spiral time means patterns repeat but always lead to growth. Now when familiar situations come around again in my life, I don't feel stuck in circles. I'm traveling a spiral path, meeting old challenges with new wisdom, revisiting familiar places from a higher perspective.

Rewild Your Soul, Reclaim Your Life, Create Something Original

In a world overwhelmed by speed, distraction, and cultural conditioning, it's easy to forget who we truly are. The mind races. The emotions pile up. And the deeper voice inside—the one longing to feel, to create, to connect—gets buried.

Whitestone WanderLust is a powerful invitation to slow down, return to the wild, and begin a sacred dialogue with the natural world. It's a nature-based journey that helps you soften the grip of the "monkey mind" and start listening to something far more ancient: the wisdom of your soul.

This is not just a walk in the woods. This is a guided return to the wilderness within.

At the heart of WanderLust is **Jeffrey Bryan Grubert**, a trained *Wild Mind* guide who draws deeply from the groundbreaking work of Bill Plotkin—particularly his books *Wild Mind: A Field Guide to the Human Psyche* and *Nature and the Human Soul*. These teachings offer a rich, nature-based framework for understanding the psyche and the Soul-Centric Wheel of Human Development—not as something broken, but as something wild, whole, and waiting to be remembered.

In WanderLust, you'll explore how nature offers a big enough space to hold the chaos of your thoughts and the weight of your feelings. The wild doesn't judge. The trees don't interrupt. The sky doesn't ask you to be anyone but who you are. And when you begin to listen, something magical happens: your emotions soften, your imagination stirs, and you begin to remember what it means to be fully alive.

To get started, below there are **10 contemplative, nature-based activities** that help you feel your feelings, meet your inner protectors, and create from the inside out. These can be done solo, in a backyard or in an open wild place. But for deeper transformation, WanderLust also offers **mentorship, online coaching, and occasional wilderness intensives** to help you mirror your experience and integrate it into your daily life.

We live in a culture that's built upon survival—on doing, achieving, proving. But everything in our culture is ultimately a reflection of the natural world. When we retreat into nature, we're not escaping. We're remembering. And we're allowing that remembrance to inform a **new way of showing up in the world**—more rooted, more creative, more authentic.

Whether you're grieving, lost, curious, or creatively blocked, WanderLust provides a sacred and grounded container to reawaken your relationship with the wild. It's about stepping away from the noise … and into your one wild and precious life.

Because here's the truth: you don't need to fix yourself. You need to *feel* yourself. And nature knows exactly how to hold you in that process. Are you ready to wander?

> "Tell me, what is it you plan to do with your one
> wild and precious life?" —Mary Oliver

10 Nature-Based Prompts for Feeling and Creating

Find a quiet, wild or semi-wild place where you can be alone. Take your journal, something to write or draw with, and an open heart. These prompts are invitations to feel your emotions, connect with nature, and create something beautiful.

1. Sit beside a tree and imagine it listening to you. Speak your feelings out loud or silently. What does the tree say in return?
2. Find a stream, river, or ocean and sit with its flow. What emotions are trying to move through you right now? Let them speak.
3. Choose a stone, leaf, or piece of bark. Hold it. What part of you does it represent? Journal about what it holds for you.
4. Lie on the earth and feel its support. Ask: what do I need to release? Breathe it into the ground. Let the earth hold it.
5. Observe something decaying, like a fallen log or dead leaf. What needs to die in you so something new can grow?
6. Watch the sky shift—clouds, sun, wind. Let it mirror your emotions. Write or draw what the sky is teaching you.
7. Find a bird or animal and watch it closely. Imagine it has a message for you. What is it here to remind you of?
8. Walk slowly, barefoot if possible. With each step, ask: what am I walking away from, and what am I walking toward?
9. Create a nature altar from found objects to honor an emotion. Photograph it or offer a prayer to the land.
10. Sit in stillness and let a song, image, or poem rise. Don't force it. Let nature inspire your next creative act.

After your wander, return home and create something—journal, draw, paint, sing, dance. Then, if you feel called, share your creation with others as a way of giving back. Try a social media post and ask for comments. The world needs your voice. Finally, if you'd like to share your offering with Whitestone, simply email whitestone320@gmail.com.

#1

#2

#3

#4

#5

Have you found your mentors and guides for your journey? If so, who are they, and how have they helped you live into your most creative authentic self? If not, are you looking?

It Takes a Village to Raise an Artist

Behind every artist stands an invisible crowd. My crowd includes: the art teacher who noticed my wild approach to a canvas. The friends who showed up in the wilderness to hold space for my birthing. The mentors who taught me art before I found my glow.

Some days, creating feels lonely—just me with a blank canvas, having a staring contest. But the truth is, my hands hold techniques taught by others. My eyes see through perspectives shared by others. My heart is created with courage built by others saying, "Keep going."

No artist is an island. We are all continents connected by bridges that others helped us build. I hope I can be a personal guide for you on your creative journey. These are a few of mine that gave birth to my unfolding. Pictured left:

#1 Gordon Grubert. Two weeks before his passing, I brought him into my studio to see this work. His response was, "I'm glad I lived long enough to see who you've become." He was a kind, gentle, and loving father who always had my back.

#2. Dwayne O'Conner. He was a good salesman, a masonry worker, an athlete, a father, a real elder for other men. At 70, he started his creative dream to carve stone. Within a year he was invited to carve at the world-famous stone artist quarry in Ventura, CA. He died of a stroke at 78, leaving his beautiful work in the world. I was lucky enough to purchase this stone carving, and it sits on my living room coffee table and keeps me inspired to do my work.

#3. Bill Ploktin was my nature-based wilderness guide for a year-long descent to soul, where I learned how to embrace my wild mind, feel everything, embrace the darkness, and begin giving something original and unique to the world. He guided me to my inner glow.

#4. Aviva Gold was my wild and wonderful medicine woman, who taught me how to transform prayer into paint, paint, paint. She travelled the world with her Painting From The Source program, helping people transform their emotions into an artistic way of life. She told me art was the trick, the process was the gold.

#5. Carioca was the medicine man that opened a light so bright inside me that I felt like I was going to die. His music and ceremony have blessed thousands of people worldwide, and he currently runs a retreat center and music school near Rio De Janeiro called Ciranda.

#6. The thousands of men and women of Alcoholics Anonymous that have provided a background for encouragement, understanding, and love for my long process of awakening. If you have a problem with substance abuse, there is a solution in the rooms of AA.

Resources

Whitestone's Resources That Help You Heal, Feel, and Create

These books changed how I relate to my mind, my emotions, and my creativity. Start with one. Let it speak to you. And if you've read something else that helped you heal, drop it in the comments—I'm always adding to the list.

1. *Wild Mind: A Field Guide to the Human Psyche* **by Bill Plotkin**
   A powerful map of the inner world, helping you understand your subpersonalities and access your wholeness through nature-based practices.

2. *Nature and the Human Soul* **by Bill Plotkin**
   This one outlines the stages of human development from a soul-centric perspective, showing how nature holds the blueprint for growing into your most authentic, creative self.

3. *The Artist's Way* **by Julia Cameron**
   A 12-week guide to recovering your creativity. Especially powerful if you're stuck or afraid to express yourself emotionally.

4. *Falling Upward* **by Richard Rohr**
   A compassionate and spiritual take on the second half of life—where we learn that loss, failure, and not knowing are actually the doorways to deeper meaning.

5. *The Body Keeps the Score* **by Bessel van der Kolk**
   For those healing emotional wounds stored in the body. Practical, research-based, and deeply validating.

6. *Painting From The Source* **by Aviva Gold**
   An easy, practical guide for painting and art philosophy that will change the world.

More on Whitestone Original Art, Prints, Merchandise, Musings, Coaching, Poetry, Books, Community

www.whitestoneglowart.com   liberations.letgotoglow.com

call.letgotoglow.com

Social Media: Whitestone YouTube: @whitestoneglowtv

Instagram: whitestone_glowart

TikTok: @whitestoneglows

Facebook: Jeffrey B. Grubert

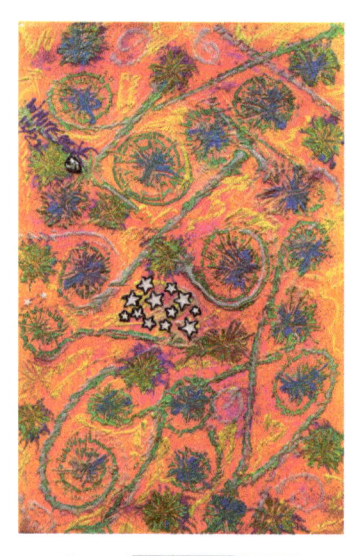

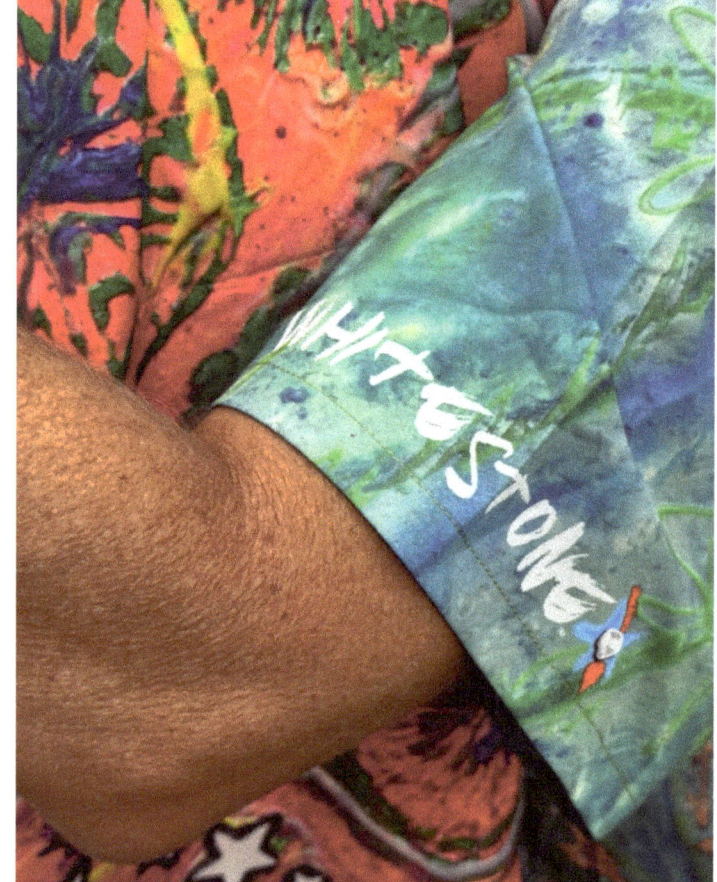

WHITESTONE'S THE ART OF LETTING GO: WEAR THE GLOW

How My Art Turned Into Shirts That Help You Remember Who You Are

When I finished writing this book, The Art of Letting Go to Glow, and just days before its final edit; something beautiful happened. I started to remember that my paintings weren't just pictures—they were full of light and sound. They were carrying a secret pattern I didn't even realize I was painting. That pattern is something called The Codex. It's a kind of invisible map made of color, music, and feeling. It helps people remember who they really are. Yes these shirts hold a vibrational resonance that helps you remember who you are! They are shirts that have a life of their own and you can feel how they ignite your own unique remembered vibration.

So I turned some of my glow art into shirts. Each shirt is like a small doorway—a portal—that carries its own special frequency. These images are the first in many that have helped me remember the unique light and frequency that I feel grateful to share with the world. That means each one has its own energy or feeling tone that you can wear, like a song you don't hear with your ears but can feel in your body.

There are four shirts in the collection, each with its own name and feeling:

- **Earth Memory – Verdant Unwinding**
- **Core Flare – Solar Emergence**
- **Night Root – Shadow Bloom**
- **Delta Drift – Liminal Passage**

When you wear these shirts, you're not just wearing color. You're wearing a part of your own memory. It's like each shirt quietly whispers to you, "Hey, you're more than you think. You're part of something big and beautiful."

Each shirt also comes with a special QR code. When you scan it, you'll hear a sound made just for that shirt. You can sit quietly with the sound, breathe, and let it help you find your own unique frequency. It's like tuning your heart back to its original song.

You can get these shirts complete with Codex Stillness Meditation Tones, while supplies last, and explore their stories at:

🌐 www.whitestoneglowart.com

Integrate Everything Within

What does it mean to integrate everything within?

Integrate Everything Within

When I painted "Integrate Everything Within," I was sitting in my old studio on a freezing winter night when suddenly my hands started moving differently. It felt like someone had switched on a light inside my brain that I didn't know was there!

Have you ever felt torn between different parts of yourself? Like the part that wants to be good and the part that sometimes feels angry or messy? That's what this painting is all about—finding a way to welcome *all* those parts.

The bright background colors—those hot oranges and electric yellows—weren't planned. They just burst out from my paint bottles like they'd been waiting to escape. I scribbled words across the canvas: "LOVE," "CURIOSITY," "GOOD," "BAD," "UGLY," "PEACE," "FORGIVE," "FLY," "GROUNDED." Each word felt like it was unlocking a door inside me that had been stuck.

I painted "YOU" in the biggest letters because I realized something huge that night—we're all connected. Your glow and my glow come from the same source. It's like we're all holding different flashlights, but the batteries come from the same package.

The happy and sad faces at the bottom? Those are reminders that it's okay to feel everything. Our feelings are like weather—they change, but the sky stays the same.

Under black light, this painting transforms completely, just like how we look different when we finally let our true selves shine. Finding your own glow isn't about being perfect. It's about being *real*—bringing together all your different pieces into one amazing, messy, beautiful whole.

What parts of yourself are you still keeping in the shadows? What might happen if you let them glow too?

It may not be my ultimate masterpiece, but I offer this graffiti art as a true expression of what drives my deepest desire to paint, write, make videos, coach, and serve with my work.

It is my hope that you will play with the ideas in this book, start some wild wandering, feel everything along the way, create something beautiful, integrate all of it, and enjoy a life that comes from *The Art of Letting Go to Glow.*

—***WHITESTONE***

www.ingramcontent.com/pod-product-compliance
Lightning Source LLC
Chambersburg PA
CBHW062025050526
44107CB00105B/933